A PASSIONATE FAITH

What makes an evangelical?

Richard Turnbull

MONARCH
BOOKS

Oxford, UK & Grand Rapids, Michigan, USA

First published in the UK in 2012 by Monarch Books
(a publishing imprint of Lion Hudson plc)
Wilkinson House, Jordan Hill Road, Oxford OX2 8DR, England
Tel: +44 (0)1865 302750 Fax: +44 (0)1865 302757
Email: monarch@lionhudson.com
www.lionhudson.com

ISBN 978 1 85424 901 2 (print)
ISBN 978 0 85721 336 5 (epub)
ISBN 978 0 85721 335 8 (Kindle)

Distributed by:
UK: Marston Book Services, PO Box 269, Abingdon, Oxon, OX14 4YN
USA: Kregel Publications, PO Box 2607, Grand Rapids, Michigan 49501

British Library Cataloguing Data
A catalogue record for this book is available from the British Library.

Printed and bound in the UK by MPG Books.

This book is dedicated to my wife, Caroline, and my children, Sarah, Katie, Matt and Rebecca.

During a period of study leave from my post as Principal of Wycliffe Hall, Oxford, a project which had begun as a study of the Evangelical Revival became not one, but two books: the story of the Revival itself (*Reviving the Heart*, Lion 2012), and this volume dealing with the spiritual heritage of the movement. I am very grateful to my editors: the commissioning editor, Tony Collins, and also Jenny Ward, without whose careful attention to detail the text would be much the poorer. I am also grateful to Monarch Books for publishing this volume, and to Katie Hofman, my personal assistant, who prepared the terms for the index.

Richard Turnbull
Oxford, Summer 2012

Revd Dr Richard Turnbull is Principal of Wycliffe Hall, Oxford and a member of the Faculty of Theology of the University of Oxford

Other publications:

Reviving the Heart: The Story of the Eighteenth Century Revival, Oxford: Lion, 2012.

Shaftesbury: The Great Reformer, Oxford: Lion, 2010.

Anglican and Evangelical?, London: Continuum, 2007 (reprinted 2010).

Contents

Introduction

Amazing grace! (how sweet the sound),
That saved a wretch like me!
I once was lost, but now am found,
Was blind, but now I see.[1]

....

These famous words of the converted slave-trader, John Newton, written in 1779 while the Rector of Olney in Buckinghamshire, told of the impact of God's grace on his life.

The verses of "Amazing Grace" have sunk deep into the Evangelical consciousness. The lyrics have also had a significant cultural impact. The grand themes of Evangelical Christianity are present – the emphases on grace, sin and conversion are all set out in the first few lines.

It seems appropriate to start a book on Evangelical spiritual origins with a hymn; hymnody has been one of the many expressions of Evangelical spirituality from the eighteenth-century Revival through to the present day. The hymn is both a vehicle for doctrine and a response of the heart to God. Evangelicalism did not invent the hymn, but has certainly used its form to convey the essence of its spiritual power.

The Evangelical movement has had an extraordinary impact upon Christian history. The roots of Evangelicalism lie in the history and theology of the Protestant Reformation; its unique experiential encounter with God (characterized today as "the personal relationship with Jesus") derives from the Awakenings in English-speaking lands in the first half of the eighteenth century. This movement has both shaped society and itself been moulded by the cultures it has operated within.

Evangelicalism is not monolithic. There are many complex patterns and a variety of historical and contemporary ingredients. Evangelicalism has also become, to some, a dirty word. This was no less true in the early days of the movement, when the epithets "saint" and "enthusiast" were not meant as terms of endearment. Today "fundamentalist" is a dismissive label that usually reveals more about the observer than the observed.

The power of Evangelicalism lies not only in its doctrine but also in its spirituality – an amorphous word, claimed by many for many things. The quest for God is an ancient one. The pursuit of the eternal has found expression in numerous religions and their spiritual traditions, from mysticism to monasticism. Definition, however, is slippery. Although the editors of *The Study of Spirituality* refer to various attempts to define spirituality, including "the forms and structures of the life of prayer" (quoting papers from a 1967 conference), they also eschew any attempt at definition themselves.[2] The matter is further complicated by recognizing that beyond the question of meaning is that of scope – spirituality can be considered not only in respect of the devotional practices of one faith, but also viewed thematically across religious traditions.

Spirituality is not the same as doctrine, but cannot be separated from confessional truth. For Evangelicals attributes such as attention to the means of prayer, communion with God and life lived in the power of the Spirit can only be authentic if they are in harmony with Christian truth as set out in the Scriptures. Nevertheless, a distinction can be drawn. The Westminster Shorter Catechism (1647) stated that "man's chief end is to glorify God, and to enjoy him for ever."[3] Richard Baxter referred to "a constant delight in God".[4] Spirituality is concerned with the means of this delight and enjoyment and its application in the life of the Christian.

The Evangelical Revival of the eighteenth century (referred to in the United States as the "Great Awakening") brought out the unique contribution of the Evangelical movement. A new energy was released and a new passion was ignited, together with a rekindled desire for God. This was manifested in many ways, some new and others the renewal of ancient expressions of Christianity. Hymns, prayer, worship and the Christian life all came into a fresh focus not as a replacement for Christian doctrine but as an expression of the heart in response to it. The Evangelicals of the Revival were concerned not only with piety and its means, but also with the Christian life. What did it mean to be called by God into discipleship? How did the continuing presence and guidance of God express itself for the Christian, indeed for the nation? Then there were the great Revival themes – not only evangelism (the spreading of the gospel), but also the transformation of society.

We will consider these questions by looking deeply into the heart of the Evangelical tradition, its piety and its practices. As the numerous strands of Evangelicalism developed, the same common spiritual heritage was articulated in different ways. In seeking to understand the various influences upon the Evangelical spiritual tradition, we will come to see why Evangelicals expressed things and acted as they did. So it is today. We will explore not only the historical roots of Evangelical spirituality but also its contemporary manifestation and practice. In doing so we will come to appreciate not only why Evangelical Christians sing, pray and respond to the divine initiative in such a diversity of ways today, but also how they seek to reclaim the power of the spiritual heritage that transformed much of English society in the eighteenth and nineteenth centuries.

My hope and prayer is that this book will build a greater understanding of our spiritual heritage and contemporary practice, not only to enhance our mutual understanding and appreciation, but more importantly to seek to focus our hearts and minds upon the spiritual rather than the political power of the Evangelical movement. Hence we may be more thoroughly equipped in the Christian life to live authentically as Christ's people.

Notes

1. Lyrics taken from the *Olney Hymnbook*, London, 1779, facsimile copy of original, Cowper and Newton Museum, Olney, 1979.
2. C. Jones, G. Wainwright and E. Yarnold, *The Study of Spirituality*, London: SPCK, 6th impression, 2004, p. xxv.
3. The Westminster Shorter Catechism, 1648, taken from Phillip Schaff, *The Creeds of Christendom*, Harper and Brothers, 1877, republished 1977, Grand Rapids, Michigan: Baker Book House.
4. Richard Baxter, dedication to *The Saints' Everlasting Rest*, quoted in G. Mursell, *English Spirituality, From Earliest Times to 1700*, London: SPCK, 2008, p. 3.

1

The Origins and Sources of Evangelical Spirituality

....

The ultimate focus of all Christian spirituality is God. To be more precise, the prime, central point of attention and affection is in the Trinitarian God, Father, Son and Holy Spirit.

For the Evangelical the way of knowing this God is through his self-revelation in two ways.

First, in the person of Jesus Christ, who is both the second person of the Trinity and the historic figure from Nazareth who walked the earth some two thousand years ago. Hence for the Evangelical, Christian spirituality cannot be separated from Christ. J. C. Ryle, the first Bishop of Liverpool (1880–1900), wrote that *"we must begin with Christ"* and we "must go to him as sinners, with no plea but that of utter need".[1]

Second, the faith to which Evangelicals adhere is that which is set out or revealed in the Holy Scriptures. It is in the Bible that we discover the true, authentic Jesus Christ. From the pages of the Bible we learn of God's character and purpose and his plan for the Christian life. For Protestant Christians, including Anglicans, this revelation in Scripture is both unique (that is, it is found nowhere else) and authoritative. It is also complete (nothing can be added) and sufficient (nothing else is needed) – topics we will return to in Chapter 2. Hence statements and affirmations about Scripture often appear in Protestant confessions of faith – the first Article of the Westminster Confession (1647) is entitled "Of Holy Scripture". It consists of ten paragraphs dealing with the Scriptures. Article 6 of the Thirty-nine Articles of the Church of England (the confessional statement of the Church of England) has the heading, "Of the sufficiency of the Holy Scriptures for salvation" and, indeed, the Anglican Declaration of Assent (taken by all ministers upon ordination and when taking a new office in the church) declares of the church, "she possesses the faith uniquely revealed in the Holy Scriptures."[2] The conclusion of these statements is that Scripture is considered the very Word of God. Hence Evangelical spirituality cannot be separated from Scripture.

The classic approach to Evangelical spirituality

Evangelical spirituality derives from the unique and significant outbreaks of "revival", mainly in Great Britain and North America, in the first half of the eighteenth century. The very concept of revival forms an important motif in Evangelical spirituality which we will consider subsequently. The origins of the revival itself are for another place,[3] but these historic events form the crucial foundation stones for considering the nature and the form of the tradition.

There are, naturally, a variety of ways of approaching Evangelical spirituality. The classic method has been to divide the Evangelical spiritual tradition into different types or streams. One characterization is "Puritan, Pietist and Pentecostalist".[4] Different terminology could be used to convey much the same meaning. So, for example, Reformed, Wesleyan and Charismatic or even Calvinist, Arminian and Revivalist might be different ways of describing the various influences. The narrative behind these alternative labels will emerge as we proceed. All such methodological approaches carry strengths and weaknesses and in this book we will look at the interaction of the differing background traditions. Nevertheless, it is widely agreed that there are three formative and distinctive traditions which shape Evangelical spirituality.

The Puritan tradition

The first of these is the Puritan (or Reformed or Calvinist) tradition. This is an appeal to the heritage of the Reformation. It is notable for a systematic approach to Scripture and doctrine, a passion for preaching, a relationship with God expressed by a covenant and a view of the Christian life which emphasizes struggle against sin and the ultimate destiny of heaven. These are the powerful themes of this Christian spiritual tradition.

This strand took its theology and name (Calvinist) from John Calvin, who was born in France in 1509 and died in Geneva in 1564. Calvin's Geneva was both an experiment in theocracy and a school of discipleship. His influence reached far and wide. He sent missionaries into his native France, gave hospitality to exiles from England and Scotland (while Mary Tudor held the throne of England and Mary Stuart that of Scotland) and trained pastors and preachers. Calvin is, of course, best known for his extraordinary work of systematic theology, the *Institutes of the Christian Religion*. This masterpiece, which repays careful reading today, was written in four books in various editions between 1536 and 1559. The work is both doctrinal and spiritual. Calvin's concern was with God, especially his majesty and his sovereignty. His passion was to "let God be God".[5] The book was enormously influential both theologically and culturally. It has affected Evangelical attitudes to life, society and the world as well as to theology and prayer.

The relationship between Calvin and his successors is one which has caused much scholarly debate. However, the groundwork which he laid allowed the doctrinal emphasis of the *Institutes* to continue to develop. Ultimately this led to the famous five points of Calvinism articulated at the Synod of Dort in 1619[6] and the idea of the covenant as the key relationship between God and his people. The Bible contains many examples of covenant. The Reformed tradition emphasizes God's unilateral action in establishing a covenant of grace through Jesus Christ. God took the initiative in the offer of salvation. However, once bestowed, this covenant can be seen in bilateral terms – the covenant of grace and the covenant of works – how a person is saved and how a person is to live. The Christian's responsibility and obedience to God has always been a significant part of this heritage.

In England the Puritan movement represented this outlook. The history of Puritanism, its relationship to both society and other Christian traditions, is complex but important for understanding Evangelical spirituality. Like so many descriptions, "Puritan" covers a wide range of thought and practice. A convenient label rarely covers a uniform outlook. Puritans in England ranged from those who operated within the spectrum of the Established Church during the reign of Elizabeth I (1558–1603), to those who advocated the abolition of the episcopate in favour of a more Presbyterian form of church government closer to Calvin's Geneva, to those who emphasized the separation of church and state.

Many Puritans wrote doctrinal works but it was often those who suffered the most persecution who penned the deepest spiritual material. Two names stand out.

John Bunyan's classic *The Pilgrim's Progress* has entered the collective consciousness far beyond the boundaries of Christianity. Bunyan's life and spirituality, notably his emphasis on the Christian's struggle, cannot be separated from his experience in the English Civil War, or wars, which decisively shaped English religious attitudes. Bunyan was born in 1628 near Bedford. He fought in the Civil War on the side of Parliament. Towards the end of the 1640s he was converted and adopted the Calvinist faith. He suffered at the time of the restoration of Charles II – the Clarendon Code imposed severe restrictions on independent preachers. Bunyan was arrested for open-air preaching. He spent the next twelve years in and out of prison. The first part of his classic work was published in 1678 and the second part in 1684, four years before his death. To the content of the work we will return in more detail in Chapter 5, but the heart of the narrative is the story of the pilgrim, Christian (a personification of Bunyan himself), who is journeying through life, facing onslaught and attack from every side. The story brings out the key themes of Puritan spirituality – the daily struggle against sin and temptation and the centrality of Scripture in guiding and shaping the Christian life.

The second name is that of Richard Baxter. Born in 1615, Baxter was the chaplain to the Parliamentary forces between 1642 and 1647, after which he held the living of

Vicar of Kidderminster. Although not the most diplomatic of people, he was passionately concerned for the spiritual health of those entrusted to him and evangelized the population of Kidderminster through door-to-door visitation. For his fellow clergy he wrote the book that became known as *The Reformed Pastor*. The kernel of this teaching was an exposition of the dual oversight of Acts 20:28 – the oversight of the self and the oversight of the flock. The book sets out the vital necessity of conversion but also deals with the work of grace in the heart that characterizes the Christian life. Baxter wrote:

> *Take heed to yourselves, lest your example contradict your doctrine, and lest you lay such stumbling blocks before the blind, as may be the occasion of their ruin; lest you unsay with your lives what you say with your tongues; and be the greatest hinderers of the success of your own labours.*[7]

The importance and strength of this strand of Evangelical spirituality is that it gives weight to doctrine and to the Reformation heritage. For this tradition doctrine and belief cannot be separated from discipleship. The Christian life is a constant battle against sin in the grace of God, a journey to a certain eternal destiny. The weakness mainly lies in recognizing that for many in this tradition assurance of heaven is frequently matched by lack of assurance in the Christian life.[8] There may also be a tendency to downplay the idea of revival due to the dominance of predestination (that is, the idea of God's sovereign choice and election of individuals for salvation or damnation) and a fear of human means, together with a degree of introspection and legality that sits somewhat ill at ease with the advocacy of God's grace.

16

The Pietist tradition

The second strand of Evangelical spirituality is often characterized as "Pietist". The word "piety" tends to convey an image of a spiritually devout person, someone perhaps earnest in prayer. The word, like "saint" and "enthusiast", has a somewhat mixed character and is sometimes used negatively. Genuine piety, however, is to be treasured. In this tradition weight is given to prayer and to the personal and even intimate nature of the individual relationship with God in Christ as Lord and Saviour.

The roots of this approach lie in the more radical elements of the sixteenth-century Reformation together with the development of continental Pietism in Germany.[9] In a desire to devote themselves more fully to Christ, believers have, at various times in Christian history, gathered themselves together in communities of the committed. This has been true across different Christian traditions from the desert fathers and medieval monasticism to the Pietist communities that concern us here. The purpose of doing so was not only to represent the purity of the church ("true believers") but also to place greater emphasis on the immediacy of the encounter with and communication with God himself. God was not just to be known about or even known, but also experienced in a daily encounter.

This tradition of Evangelical spirituality was one of the important backdrops to the Revival of the eighteenth century. Among the key personalities to emerge from this recovery of Pietism's spiritual vitality were John and Charles Wesley. The Wesleys were not alone in the early decades of the eighteenth century in seeking to recover the idea of holiness of life. The vibrancy of the Puritan tradition had somewhat subsided but spiritual hunger continued amid a period of time seen by some as spiritually dark but by others as a period of continued spiritual depth.[10]

John Wesley, motivated during his time in Oxford by this spiritual desire, came into contact with a group of Moravians while he was travelling to the colony of Georgia. This particular group originated from Germany, standing in succession to some of the Anabaptist communities of the Radical Reformation (see Chapter 2). These groups had emerged in the latter part of the seventeenth century under the influence of continental Pietism (with an emphasis on experience and encounter of God). They had rather "kept a candle burning", in other words, maintained a witness for the idea of the experience of God in the life of the believer. One community, formed on the estates of Count Nicholas von Zinzendorf, was known as Herrnhut. In the England of the late seventeenth and early eighteenth centuries, whatever the scholarly opinion as to the nature of faith, there was an increasing desire to meet with God. The question was "how" this was achieved.

The Wesleyan tradition is an important part of the Evangelical spiritual heritage which will feature further as we progress. The key point, summarized by Wesley himself, demonstrates its distinctive nature. Religion, he said,

> ... *is not barely a speculative, rational thing, a cold life-less asset, a train of ideas in the head, but also a disposition of the heart.*[11]

Although the criticism may be somewhat unfair, the Puritans were often seen as cold and rationalistic, whereas the Wesleyans were perceived as warm and intuitive. Inevitably this approach emphasizes some elements of spirituality which are not so central in the Reformed model. The desire for all to be able to meet with God, to encounter him in the heart and to be transformed, became a characteristic of much of what was later known as the Wesleyan Methodist tradition.

This carried with it enormous strengths. God was a reality with whom an individual relationship was possible. Pietists gave emphasis in their life and worship to the utter devotion of the heart to God, attaching significantly greater weight to the experiential encounter with the Almighty.

However, some of the theology that lay behind these Pietistic communities was somewhat problematic and continued to be so from an Evangelical perspective. The original communities tended to be separatist. In other words, in their desire to represent the community of pure believers, the Pietists often viewed the world as an evil and dirty place, to be shunned. This was in sharp contrast to the Magisterial Reformers (the leading Reformation figures such as Luther, Zwingli and Calvin) and the later Puritans who saw the world more as a place of discipleship, even a school. Although the more extreme aspects of separatism were overcome in the Evangelical Revival, this quest for purity led to assumptions about Christian perfection in this world that many saw as failing to give due weight to the reality of sin. If the Puritan encounter was with sin and its reality, then the Pietist encounter was with God himself.

A further difficulty lay in the fact that Wesley followed Jacob Arminius (1560–1609) in his theology rather than John Calvin. Although some of the nuances of this are easily lost on us today, the debate, in essence, was whether the atoning sacrifice of Jesus was effective for all (Arminius) or only for the elect (Calvin). Did God predestine to salvation his elect or did all of humanity have the freedom of the will to respond?

Naturally, the impulse of revival encouraged those who thought that all may be saved by an act of will in response to the preaching of the new birth necessary in Christ. Nevertheless, Calvinism remained an important feature of the Evangelical Revival, especially within the Church of England.

The Pentecostalist tradition

The third strand of Evangelical spirituality is often described as Pentecostalist. Historically, this is somewhat misleading and even anachronistic. The modern Pentecostalist movement did not begin until the early years of the twentieth century and neo-Pentecostalism (in the form of the Charismatic movement) not until some time after the close of the Second World War. There were, however, antecedents, notably the development of the holiness movement within Evangelicalism in the second half of the nineteenth century, which took the traditional Pietism a stage further. The holiness movement had a profound impact on the spiritual life of Christians and mainstream Evangelicalism. The Keswick Convention and a great deal of the hymnody which derived from the latter part of the reign of Queen Victoria owe their origins to this movement. Keswick, a town nestling in the Lake District of northern England, was the location for an annual gathering of Evangelical Christians from 1875 (see Chapter 5). Although this was not "Pentecostalism before Pentecostalism", some, though not all, of the theological and cultural emphases prepared the way for later developments. We will consider the effect of this in Chapters 5 and 6. A further element was the "revivalist" movement, which itself had a long history, and which we will look at in some detail in Chapter 7. Both these developments were deeply influenced by the Victorian traditions of Romanticism.

If Puritanism emphasized doctrine and Pietism the believer's relationship with Christ, then the holiness movement and the wider revivalism was characterized by the experiential. God was not only to be known and encountered but experienced as a daily reality as the Lord of life. Some of these distinctions are subtle but in terms of the spiritual life, the holiness movement gave weight to the idea of an active divine providence (God's active oversight of the life of the believer), the reality of revival and God's action in the world. It moved the experience of an encounter with God from simple intimacy to heightened emotion.

The theological weakness of aspects of this movement was that it took ideas of "higher sanctification" (the Christian quest for the higher life of holiness) and "second blessing" (the filling of the Spirit after conversion) in a direction which further departed from the classic tradition. Experience is always central to Evangelical faith. The problems arise when experience becomes a key distinguishing mark of the spiritual relationship with God in its own right. The crucial danger at this point is failure to give due weight to the two determining features of any Evangelical spirituality – Christ and the Bible.

Doctrine and practice

Too much can be made of the division of the Evangelical movement into logical, neat streams, convenient for the historian or commentator but of only limited use in seeking the core of the faith. Similarly, it is not just a rather crude combining of these different background traditions that gives Evangelicalism its spiritual heart. All of these elements have strengths and weaknesses. The value lies in understanding *how* these aspects come together. So the heart of the Evangelical spirit is not that some people emphasize doctrine and others encounter with Christ or experience of God; but rather that the core of the movement involves experiencing and encountering the person and the truth of God. The diagram below first appeared elsewhere,[12] and, in slightly amended form, is a useful illustration of the influence of these various elements of Evangelical spirituality.

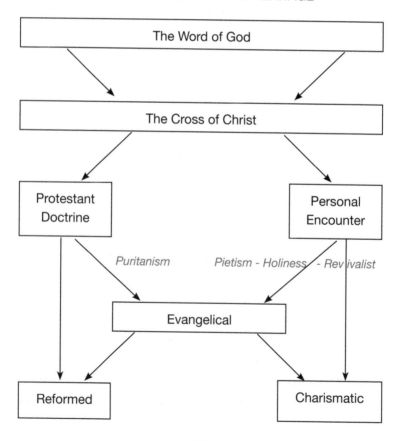

EVANGELICAL SPIRITUAL HERITAGE

The Word of God

The Cross of Christ

Protestant Doctrine

Personal Encounter

Puritanism   *Pietism - Holiness - Revivalist*

Evangelical

Reformed

Charismatic

Two things lie at the centre of the Evangelical spiritual tradition: the Word of God and the cross of Christ. The Christian understanding of the work of Christ on the cross derives from the authority of Scripture. The Word and the cross need to be encountered as both doctrine and reality. Through them we learn truth, relationship, intimacy and sacrifice. In this way we are equipped both for the Christian life and for Christian witness. These central, core spiritual realities also evoke responses in our heart, from hymn and song to sacrificial discipleship and service.

Clearly, Christians will display differing emphases in their life and practice. Some will place particular weight upon doctrinal truth, others upon experience. In understanding contemporary spirituality and practice, the Charismatic understanding of the Christian life is most strongly influenced by those sources of encounter, personal relationship, experience and power. The Reformed, by contrast, place greater weight on doctrine, truth, discipleship alongside personal relationship. The key to appreciating current practice is to recognize that all of these various influences are mediated through the Word and the person of Christ, by the Spirit, without which Evangelicalism loses either its roots or its power. So it is possible to seek to emphasize Protestant doctrine without it being mediated through personal encounter and relationship with the divine. This can lead to nationalistic Protestantism (as represented, for example, by the Orange Order in Northern Ireland). Doctrine and identity become so entwined that there is much danger of losing the heart of the gospel.

Similarly, at the Charismatic end of the spectrum, attempts to mediate spiritual reality and truth unrelated to the doctrines of the Word and of Christ can result in a spirituality of the New Age rather than anything which is authentically Evangelical. The Pietist/holiness axis can also step outside the mainstream with a revivalism that has all the hallmarks of programme and method but has lost its divine content, and quite possibly Christian truth with it. Some expressions of spirituality may find themselves somewhere on, or beyond, the margins in this diagram. In these cases we should exercise great caution. One example would be the "emerging church" movement where there has been a tendency to embrace ideas and concepts that depart from Evangelical spiritual truth. A second illustration would be how Protestant Christians relate spiritually to Roman Catholicism and Catholic spiritual practices, which can be an expression of a powerful unity in the Spirit (at one end of the spectrum), or a sad departure from traditional beliefs (at the other).

A recognition of the range of Evangelical spirituality helps us understand why Evangelical Christian disciples express their faith in complementary, albeit different ways. For the more Reformed, proclamation, doctrine, teaching and truth are dominant themes. Hymnody expresses doctrine. Worship is likely to have a degree of simplicity, avoiding too much ceremonial, and centred on Christ and the Word. Prayer is ordered and intercessory, emphasizing God's character as well as personal need. For the more Charismatic, intimacy, experience of God, surrender to him, and expressing love for him all feature. There may, in some elements of the tradition, be an emphasis on spiritual power, including characteristics such as words of prophecy, speaking in tongues and other related phenomena. Prayer may be more active and intimate, even physical and perhaps emotional.

In summary, it is crucial to recognize a number of things.

First, a distinction needs to be drawn between style and theology. There are some theological differences on this continuum of spirituality concerning how God relates to his people and the nature of revelation. These divergences should not be underestimated but we should also recognize that a significant amount of the diversity reflects variations in temperament and style. Not every difference of expression in Evangelical spirituality should be viewed as a theological divide.

Second, key aspects of our spirituality as Evangelicals draw from the strength of all of these different elements. Two examples will suffice. Discipleship is a central element of Evangelical life and practice. To be an effective disciple for Christ requires the guidance of the Word, a living relationship with Christ and a surrender of the will to God. Similarly, the way in which the Evangelical relates to society requires confidence in the public nature of Christian faith and doctrine and the willing sacrifice of one's all to God's service. These aspects of Christian discipleship cannot be simply explained by a fixed point on a spectrum. Rather, there is a continuum. Much of the diversity can be explained by the varying degrees of weight placed at different points.

Third, the Word of God and the person of Christ are central. If we can understand the differences in method and approach that make up the Evangelical tradition, then we can avoid drawing conclusions about doctrine from style. However, to be effective as Evangelical witnesses we need to understand the absolute bedrock which is formed by the Word of God in Scripture and the person of Christ who died on the cross. Without those elements the Evangelical faith is nothing. The Holy Spirit mediates the Word and the relationship with Christ into the reality of the daily Christian life.

We have established, then, something of the nature of the sources of Evangelical spirituality; we now need to explore further and deeper the key elements of our spiritual life and practice.

Notes

1. J. C. Ryle, *Holiness*, London: James Clark & Co., 1956, p. 32.
2. Richard Turnbull, *Anglican and Evangelical?*, London: Continuum, 2007 (reprinted 2010), pp. 22, 41.
3. Richard Turnbull, *Reviving the Heart: The Story of the Eighteenth Century Revival*, Oxford: Lion, 2012.
4. John Tiller, *Puritan, Pietist, Pentecostalist: Three Types of Evangelical Spirituality*, Nottingham: Grove Books, 1982.
5. The *Institutes* cover a wide range of theological themes including God as Creator and Redeemer, election and predestination and the doctrine of the church, ministry and sacraments.
6. TULIP – Total depravity, Unconditional election, Limited atonement, Irresistible grace, Perseverance of the saints.
7. Richard Baxter, *The Reformed Pastor*, 1.3, Banner of Truth, p. 63.
8. David Bebbington, *Evangelicalism in Modern Britain*, London: Unwin Hyman, 1989, pp. 42–45.
9. Turnbull, *Reviving the Heart*.
10. See, for example, J. C. D. Clark, *English Society 1688–1832*, Cambridge: CUP, 1985.
11. Wesley, *Works*, vii, 9–10 (Sermon on Salvation by Faith), quoted in J. D. Walsh, "Origins of the Evangelical Revival" in G. V. Bennett and J. D. Walsh (eds), *Essays in Modern Church History*, London: A&C Black, 1966, p. 149.
12. Richard Turnbull, *Anglican and Evangelical?*, p. 80.

2

The Bible: Proclamation and Response

....

The Evangelical doctrine of Scripture has been well rehearsed elsewhere.[1] Our concern here is with the understanding of Scripture primarily as it impacts upon the spiritual life of the believer. However, the spiritual consequences cannot be separated from the doctrinal position. For Evangelicals spirituality flows from doctrine and not vice versa. In essence, Evangelicals believe in the authority of Scripture, its inspiration and its infallibility. This understanding is neither a recent assertion nor simply a reaction to claims of papal infallibility or the advance of rationalism in the nineteenth century. There is an important and positive heritage to the authority and centrality of the Word in Evangelicalism.

At the end of the eighteenth century the early Evangelical leaders in England gathered together in a debating group known as the Eclectic Society. They were under no illusion as to the nature of Scripture, its authority and inspiration.[2] The inspiration was not just general ("God guided the authors") but also plenary and verbal ("God gave the authors the words"). However, this did not mean that the hard work of interpretation could be avoided. The task of understanding and explaining Scripture goes back over many centuries: it did not arise only as new literary, historical and theological methodologies emerged. Authentic Evangelical devotion requires a faithful, as well as a humble, understanding of Scripture. As we shall see, the spiritual point is not just that Scripture is authoritative but also that it is sufficient and complete, has transforming power and is intended for preaching and proclamation.

To begin with we need to consider the nature of Scripture. Does the written Word have authority in itself, or is the text simply a witness to the true and living Word, Jesus Christ? It is fashionable in some Evangelical circles to emphasize the text as witness. This has been reinforced by loss of confidence in the Bible as the Word of God and loss of historical perspective within the Evangelical spiritual tradition. It is not only Evangelicals who would maintain that the person of Christ lies at the centre of our faith and that the Scriptures witness to him. However, for Evangelicals, the Bible does not simply function as witness. Historic Evangelical spiritual teaching is that the text itself carries authority, the words of Scripture have transformational power, and the teaching of Scripture must be obeyed. This goes some considerable way beyond simply treating the Bible as a witness to a greater reality in Christ. The separation of the written Word from the living Word is not a division that the forebears of the Evangelical faith would recognize.

How has this separation arisen and how can we recover an appropriate spirituality of Scripture? First, we need a greater appreciation of the Reformed doctrine of the *perspicuity* of Scripture. Perspicuity essentially refers to the way in which Scripture contains a clear and accessible message. For the Evangelical, Scripture belongs in the hands of the believer. Even before the Reformation, John Wycliffe articulated the nature of perspicuity. As well as affirming the truth of Scripture, he also asserted that its power lay in the accessibility of these truths by the ordinary person.[3] In essence this means two things. First, that Scripture contains a clear message. Second, that message is discernible and capable of being understood by the ordinary individual reading the Bible. These principles in themselves are key drivers behind the availability of Scripture in the vernacular and the work of Bible translation. In the medieval church the Bible and its interpretation had become the property of the professionals, the priests, and the institution, the church, who acted not only as the guardians, but also as the ultimate interpreters. We may think we have moved beyond this. However, we do need to exercise a degree of caution, since Reformed and Evangelical spirituality has always been susceptible to replacing one hierarchical or ecclesiastical authority with another one (the authoritative preacher or commentary or the received tradition). Indeed, and in response to this problem, some radicals then and since have eschewed all ecclesiastical offices (and hence have adopted other boundary markers, such as believers' baptism).

Contemporary Evangelical spirituality has lost sight of perspicuity, because of its tendency to heavy dependence on theories of interpretation and professional commentary. This has had the impact of loosening the place of private judgment, which is a linked and important characteristic alongside perspicuity. Private judgment refers to the ability of the individual to read, expound and test the text of Scripture. It does not mean that any one individual interpretation, or bizarre notion, is invested with authority. Modern Evangelical spirituality has lost sight of the importance of private judgment. In the nineteenth century, the prominent

Evangelical leader, the Earl of Shaftesbury, noted that "tens of thousands have thrown off their corrupt and ignorant faith… simply and solely from reading the Word of God, pure and unadulterated, without note or comment."[4] In 1860, responding to more liberal trends, Shaftesbury rounded on those who argued that the Bible could only be understood by the learned.[5] Evangelical spirituality will wish to affirm open Bibles, accessibility, shared insight, the plain meaning of the text, the clarity of Scripture and mutual accountability under God.

The Bible not only carries authority. It is also *sufficient*. The concept of the sufficiency of Scripture has faded into insignificance (or occasionally misinterpretation) yet is crucial for our spiritual understanding of Scripture. The sufficiency of Scripture means that the Bible contains everything we need in order to know God, to know his will, to obey him and to receive salvation. It is well summarized for us in Article 6 of the Church of England's Thirty-nine Articles, entitled, "Of the Sufficiency of the holy Scriptures for salvation". The opening line is: "Holy Scripture containeth all things necessary to salvation…"[6] This Article is sometimes misinterpreted as meaning that Scripture is only inspired or authoritative in respect of matters pertaining to salvation. This is not so. The Article asserts the *sufficiency* of Scripture. In other words, there is nothing else needed for faith and belief beyond what is in Scripture. The inspiration and authority of all of Scripture is well attested within the Anglican tradition.[7] Article 6 helpfully expands on the idea of sufficiency. Only that which is in Scripture or may be proved by Scripture is accepted as an article of faith or as necessary for salvation. Hence there is nothing additional, nothing ecclesiastical nor spiritual, nothing based on tradition or rationality or experience which is needed alongside Scripture.

The concept of sufficiency does not mean that the Bible answers every question or covers every situation. Well-attested Reformed concepts such as "adiaphora" (things indifferent) and Richard Hooker's argument that when Scripture is silent a variety of practice is permitted (the justification for the use of the church calendar) reinforce the concept of the sufficiency of Scripture in matters of faith and salvation. The quest is for unity in all things essential, diversity in all things non-essential.

Spiritually this is all very important. As Evangelicals we are to look nowhere outside of Scripture for our faith and practice and we are to be obedient to what Scripture teaches. We are not to be tempted by mystical or ceremonial or other ecclesiastical practices which contradict the faith and doctrine of Scripture. Spiritually that approach is essential so that matters of doctrine and salvation are not compromised. However, that does not mean that the Bible is a technical instruction manual to be read like a reference book. Rather, the Word of God is a living, powerful, sufficient and transforming Word. The inward illumination of the Holy Spirit is needed for the Word to be effective for salvation.

Closely allied to the concept of sufficiency, and equally important in understanding spiritually the nature of Scripture, is the idea that Scripture is also *complete*. This is somewhat controversial in contemporary Evangelicalism and historically has been challenged by some of the more radical Evangelical traditions. The concept has also been misused at various times for polemical purposes. So it is important we are very clear about what is and what is not meant by the idea, as well as setting out the spiritual implications. The doctrine of the completeness of Scripture teaches us that

God's Word is complete, that it represents the sum total of God's divinely inspired revelation to us. Scripture cannot be added to in any way. Sufficiency and completeness are two sides of the same coin. One teaches that Scripture contains all we need; the other that nothing can be added or taken away. The completeness of Scripture means first that there can be no new revelation from God. Some Evangelicals find this difficult and wish to assert a primacy to the Spirit. We will return to the implications of this discussion shortly, but setting aside debate over the nature of the Spirit's action in the life of the believer, what we can say with confidence is that Evangelical spirituality asserts no new definitive revelation. That does not mean that God, through his Word, illuminated by his Spirit, does not speak to believers today. Rather, it is a protection against heresy and against an excessive subjective spiritualization ("the Spirit has spoken") and internalizing ("the Spirit has spoken to me") of the Word of God.

We need to dwell here a little longer because this is a contested area (or perhaps better, a much misunderstood aspect of Evangelical spirituality in relation to the Bible). We will consider the Bible's life-transforming power across the Evangelical spiritual traditions shortly. However, we should note at this point the line of heritage in which this aspect of Evangelical spirituality has been challenged.

At the time of the sixteenth-century Reformation, there was a radical wing (known to historians and theologians as "the Radical Reformation") which formed separatist communities of faithful believers. These Anabaptist (that is, "re-baptizers") groups largely came about through applying Scripture against the leaders of what was known as the Magisterial Reformation (that is, reform achieved through the civic magistrate), as represented by many of the well-known names, including Martin Luther, John Calvin and the Zurich Reformer, Huldrych Zwingli. In effect the sheep turned against the shepherds and challenged the leadership to take their view of Scripture to its logical conclusions.

There were various groups. The more moderate, the Anabaptists, simply wanted to give weight to certain scriptural demands that were inconvenient for the likes of Zwingli (primarily, believers' baptism). However, the more radical communities effectively spiritualized the Word of God and internalized it, so that the Spirit assumed a primacy. Hence provision was made within these groups for dreams, visions, prophecies, and other extra-biblical revelations. The crucial debate is not whether God can act in this way, but what authority should be given to such phenomena. That is what divided the radicals and the moderates even within the Radical Reformation. These groups were the antecedents of the Pietistic communities that formed in Germany in the early eighteenth century (mentioned in Chapter 1) who sought that elusive personal encounter with God. They also form part of the backdrop to some aspects of the later holiness tradition and its concept of surrender to God (for more details see Chapter 5), especially its more radical revivalism. These later came to find fuller expression in the Pentecostal and Charismatic spiritual traditions.

So we can trace a line from the Radicals to some elements of contemporary spirituality concerning the way in which God acts. Historically, as we will see, some elements of these developments were absorbed into mainstream Evangelical spirituality, while others remained marginal. In some instances these spiritual developments were characterized by the return of the Pentecostal gifts, especially speaking in tongues, but also gifts of healing and prophecy, the so-called supernatural gifts. The doctrine of the completeness of Scripture makes no comment on the propriety or otherwise of these spiritual practices for the edification of the church and the believer but does assert that they cannot carry authoritative revelation. Some Evangelical spiritual traditions, as noted above, may reflect many of these practices, but they should not be invested with an authority which they cannot carry.

Those Evangelicals who have most jealously guarded the completeness of Scripture have also sometimes misunderstood it. This has been the case when a particularly narrow version of what is known as "dispensationalism" is imposed upon the narrative of the New Testament. According to this view the completeness of Scripture demands the closure of the canon of Scripture at the end of the apostolic age and concludes that the supernatural gifts are extinct. This is because dispensationalism views history as divided into certain eras or dispensations. The key to understanding the concept is to recognize that God acts in a different way in each dispensation. There is some merit in this approach, but a rigorous application of and policing of the boundaries between dispensations leads to a rigidity that goes beyond what is warranted from Scripture and is a misunderstanding of the nature of the completeness of Scripture.

How then should we understand the supernatural activities recorded in the pages of the New Testament? Are these practices – healings, exorcisms, tongues-speaking, words of knowledge, prophecy and so forth – to be replicated as normative in the contemporary age or are these activities relevant to the apostolic age only? What authority do they carry?

The first key boundary marker to recognize is that the completeness of Scripture means that no new *authoritative* revelation is possible. Second, that the miracles, healings and prophetic utterances of the New Testament were of a different order from such phenomena in later times. Third, there is the recognition of the continuing action of God in the world today through his Spirit. A reasonable conclusion to draw is that the expected replication of such phenomena or gifts is not normative, but equally is not excluded spiritually. As we have noted, there are Evangelical spiritual traditions which have a long heritage of giving some weight to these spiritual practices. However, an excessive concern with the phenomena could be seen as on, or even beyond, the margins of authentically Evangelical spirituality.

So, alongside perspicuity, we can set sufficiency and now completeness of Scripture. Taking these three ideas together, we can gain a deeper insight into Evangelical spiritual practices as they relate to our understanding of Scripture.

The transforming power of the Word

Evangelicals are united in seeing the Word of God as not only an objective, written Word, but also a spiritually transforming Word. This has significant implications for devotion, for life and for preaching, and helps explain the priorities accorded to these elements of Evangelical spirituality. The recognition of the Bible as spiritually transforming illustrates that it is the Word which has power. The Word becomes personal to the individual. This combination of *power* and *personalization* (that is, the individual discovers and accepts the power of the Bible, ingests it and grows spiritually and so is motivated and equipped) makes the Word ready for proclamation. This is the essential explanation for the centrality of preaching within Evangelical spirituality. The preaching of the Word of God will change lives.

How then does the Bible function for the convert devotionally? Spiritually it is the action of the Holy Spirit in the heart of the disciple that brings about both the power of the Word and its individual application to the life of the believer. Bruce Hindmarsh has noted that the "experience of a text of Scripture being made personal ('applied to me') recurred frequently in evangelical conversions".[8] Among various examples, he records a convert from the Cambuslang revival of 1741–42 saying that in their pre-conversion state they had never felt the Word of God coming home in power.[9] By implication that is exactly how they would describe the impact of the Word after conversion.

One consequence of this is the priority accorded to the meditative, prayerful study of Scripture. One of the leading Evangelical leaders towards the end of the eighteenth century was Charles Simeon of Cambridge (1759–1836). Simeon was converted in 1779 (see Chapter 3) and became the Vicar of Holy Trinity, Cambridge and a mentor to preachers and candidates to ordination. Simeon worked hard at Bible study in the early mornings, "studying the Holy Scriptures and meditating upon them in such a way that their truths sank into the depths of his personality, and moulded him into the mature Christian character he became."[10] According to one visitor, this meant getting up at 4 a.m. and giving the first four hours of the day to prayer and the devotional reading of Scripture.[11] Simeon, unsurprisingly, remained unmarried. He remarked that we must search the Scriptures for "hid treasures, and lay up in our hearts, yea in our inmost souls the glorious truths which they unfold to our view."[12] In this way the truth of Scripture does not simply remain a lifeless affirmation, but becomes spiritually transforming to heart and soul.

John Wesley showed a similar approach, albeit with some different emphases. He was nothing if not methodical and precise. Rather bizarrely, he even recorded in his diaries his daily activities marked on a numerical scale according to his self-perceived "grace rating". For Wesley, Scripture was not only the place of divine truth, but also a guidebook. He illustrated the transforming power of Scripture with his comment that "The Spirit of God not only once inspired those who wrote it, but continually inspires, supernaturally assists, those who read it with earnest prayer."[13] Through reading and absorbing Scripture the Christian receives divine guidance and assistance. This reflects the spiritual and personal nature of Scripture to the Evangelical and, of course, is also an essential prelude to the exploration of divine providence to which we will turn in Chapter 4. Wesley recommended – at least to one correspondent – two hours daily of Bible reading and he reflected the standard Evangelical practice of taking time out on his own from his busy life to meditate on Scripture only with the presence of God.

All the early divines also read Scripture in a deeply devotional way and not just for knowledge or information. The aim was the conforming of the heart, life and mind to the image of Christ. Hannah More (1745–1833), one of several women prominent in the Revival, as well as referring to Scripture as "nutriment to the heart",[14] interestingly also commented that "the beauty of Scripture consists of pronouns".[15] This is a very early example of how Evangelicals personalized – or, being more critical, individualized – the faith. George Whitefield (1714–70), with Wesley, probably the most prominent of the early Evangelicals, added that the "scriptures contain the deep things of God, and therefore can never be sufficiently searched into by a careless, superficial, cursory way of reading them, but by an industrious, close and humble application."[16]

Family devotions were also important and became characteristic in the households of later Evangelicals such as Wilberforce. Evangelicalism was the religion of the home. Henry Thornton, one of the Clapham group, wrote that it "is through the institution of families that the knowledge of God and of his laws is handed down from generation to generation."[17] In aristocratic circles household prayers would include the servants. There was a variety of practice here with a resistance to long homilies. Regularity was essential. It was the responsibility of the father, as head of the household, to bring a Scripture reading before the family, to have studied the commentaries and then relate the reading to the news of the day. The Wilberforce household seems to have had around ten minutes of prayer each evening at about quarter to ten, read by William, "very slowly in a low, solemnly awful voice".[18] Later a period of morning prayer and hymn singing was introduced.[19] The key was devotional attachment to Scripture and not just intellectual understanding. Indeed, at the end of the eighteenth century, William Goode warned at the Eclectic Society against the temptation of "degenerating from the devotional into the critical".[20]

We can see the regular themes of both individualization (the personal Word) and personalization (the personal Word with spiritual power for me) in Evangelical approaches to Scripture. For the Evangelical the Scriptures do not function just intellectually or liturgically but devotionally and personally. Hence individual engagement with the text of Scripture, with the heart turned to God, lay at the root of the spiritually powerful and transformative Word of God. In the sermon, this power was applied to others. In revival the hearers responded.

The Bible proclaimed and preached: the centrality of the sermon

Sermons both before and after the Evangelical Revival were long and their titles often longer still, so there clearly was no direct connection between length and effect! How then did the early Evangelicals view the proclamation of the Bible and the place of the sermon?

The sermon was the appointed means by which the power of the Word of God was brought to bear upon the hearts of the hearers. The purpose was primarily to invite repentance and the preaching of the "new birth" was a significant feature of the Revival. Clearly, there were instructional or teaching aspects to preaching, but there was much Evangelical resistance to the old-fashioned practice of sermons that were doctrinally orthodox (and *very* long) but extraordinarily dry.

The Eclectic Evangelicals at the end of the eighteenth century saw three aspects to preaching – doctrinal, experiential and practical, covering the mind, the heart and life. Again we see here the importance for Evangelical spirituality of the Word made both personal and practical.

Sermons did carry responsibility for conveying Christian truth and doctrine. The Eclectics expressed some concern at the decline of, or loss of, doctrinal preaching ("we are often defective in not stating Doctrine. People are lamentably ignorant even after hearing for twenty years").[21] Whitefield, however, was noted for the stress he placed on the heart – though this was an emphasis that sat alongside, rather than replacing doctrine. One convert noted that Whitefield "makes less of doctrine than our American preachers generally do, and aims more at affecting the heart"[22] – the American colonies had become rather renowned for a very sound, but particularly tedious Presbyterianism. Another noted that "hearing him preach, gave me a heart wound", though also noted his Calvinist doctrine.[23] Whitefield proclaimed in one sermon, "I shall return home with a heavy heart, unless some of you arise and come to my Jesus… why may he not call some of you, out of these despised fields."[24] He wrote, on another occasion, "My brethren, the word is near you. Search the scriptures. Beg of God to make you willing to be saved in this day of power",[25] and again, "Had I less love for your souls, I might speak less. But that love of God, which is shed abroad in my heart, will not permit me to leave you till I see whether you will come to Christ or no."[26] Whitefield's sermons were in fact deeply doctrinal, with themes including repentance, justification, the Christian life, the nature of Christ and so on. He did not avoid hard topics, hell included: "now then, for God's sake, for your own soul's sake, if ye have a mind to dwell with God and cannot bear the thought of dwelling in everlasting burning…"[27]

Whitefield was not alone. In Massachusetts one of Jonathan Edwards' most famous sermons was "Sinners in the Hands of an Angry God". This combination of intellect and emotion, clearly founded in confidence in God and his Word and with a degree of prominence given to preaching for repentance and new birth, came to mark out the spirituality of preaching for Evangelicals.

There were also implications for content and style. The

early Evangelicals began with the text of Scripture itself; sometimes a passage and on other occasions a verse. Noll refers to Whitefield's characteristic practice of announcing and reading a text of Scripture followed by audible (but sometimes also silent) prayer and then his sermon.[28] There was some resistance to preaching through lengthy extracts, books of the Bible or consecutive passages. This was probably in reaction to "dry orthodoxy" but also reflected something of the revivalist culture and atmosphere (see Chapter 7). However, the Bible was to speak for itself – the Earl of Shaftesbury famously referred to the Bible as its own missionary. Simeon, in the heat of the controversies between Wesley and Whitefield over doctrine,[29] and himself the author of 2,536 sermon outlines, studiously avoided advocating any theological or doctrinal system simply to expound the text. The objective, according to Simeon, was to "bring out of scripture what is there, and not to thrust in what I think might be there."[30] Unity, clarity and perspicuity were the essential characteristics – there could be no greater simplicity of message than the new birth offered in Christ.

Evangelicals tend to assume in contemporary practice that a long sermon is a good one, or at the very least, a distinguishing mark of Evangelical spirituality. This itself is probably something of a reaction to the reduction of sermon length (and evacuation of sermon content) in a great deal of post-war preaching across the denominations. The preaching of the Revival was itself something of a reaction to the prevailing customs of the time, albeit in the opposite direction – preachers tended to preach shorter sermons than was the norm. Shorter, of course, does not mean short! A reduction, however, from two or three hours to one hour was a more characteristic feature. The hearts of many had been deadened by long and complex, even if orthodox, sermons. John Newton, after his first sermon as Rector of Olney in 1764, commented that "I was thought too long, too loud, too much extempore."[31]

What was the result of all this preaching? The leaders of the Revival viewed God as actively at work in the heart of the believer and more broadly. It was the combination of the spiritual power of the Word and its proclamation that led to revival. The entire event was a work of the Spirit. So, Whitefield remarked in 1742, "I believe there is such a work begun, as neither we nor our fathers have heard of", and Jonathan Edwards said, "we live in a day wherein God is doing marvellous things".[32] Revival was the context in which the spiritually powerful, transformative Word of God was brought to bear upon the repentant hearts of significant numbers of people, through the divinely appointed means of preaching. We will investigate this further in Chapter 7.

Wesley preached some 40,000[33] sermons in his life, Whitefield perhaps 30,000.[34] No doubt some were repeats! What was new in the preaching was the bringing together of doctrine and experience, intellect and emotion, centred upon the need for repentance and new birth. These distinctive features became the characteristics of Evangelical preaching.[35] Doctrine was not optional, but essential, yet doctrine without the new birth was useless.

Notes

....

1. See, for example, Richard Turnbull, *Anglican and Evangelical?*, London: Continuum, 2007 (reprinted 2010), pp. 59–65.
2. Turnbull, *Anglican and Evangelical?*, pp. 59–65.
3. A. Kenny (ed.), *Wycliffe in his Times*, Oxford: Clarendon Press, 1986, p. 4.
4. Richard Turnbull, *Shaftesbury: The Great Reformer*, Oxford: Lion, 2010, p. 214.
5. Turnbull, *Shaftesbury*, p. 214.
6. Article 6, Thirty-nine Articles of Religion, annexed to the Book of Common Prayer.
7. Turnbull, *Anglican and Evangelical?*, pp. 36–46.
8. D. Bruce Hindmarsh, *The Evangelical Conversion Narrative*, Oxford: OUP, 2005, p. 83.
9. Hindmarsh, *The Evangelical Conversion Narrative*, p. 201.
10. Michael Hennell and Arthur Pollard (eds), *Charles Simeon (1759–1836)*, London: SPCK, 1959, p. 29.
11. James Gordon, *Evangelical Spirituality*, London: SPCK, 1991, p. 102.
12. Hennell and Pollard, *Simeon*, p. 30.
13. John Wesley, quoted in Gordon, *Evangelical Spirituality*, p. 35.
14. Gordon, *Evangelical Spirituality*, p. 113.
15. Gordon, *Evangelical Spirituality*, p. 113.
16. George Whitefield, quoted in Gordon, *Evangelical Spirituality*, p. 61.
17. Henry Thornton, quoted in D. Rosman, *Evangelicals and Culture*, Beckenham: Croon Helm, 1984, p. 97.
18. The Farington Diary, 19 July 1806, quoted in D. Newsome, *The Parting of Friends*, London: John Murray, 1966, p. 33.
19. Newsome, *The Parting of Friends*, p. 34.
20. J. H. Pratt, *The Thought of the Evangelical Leaders*, 1856, Edinburgh: Banner of Truth Trust, 1978, p. 194.
21. Pratt, *The Thought of the Evangelical Leaders*, p. 79.
22. Mark Noll, *The Rise of Evangelicalism*, Leicester: Apollos, 2004, p. 98.
23. Noll, *The Rise of Evangelicalism*, p. 99.
24. Lee Gatiss (ed.), *The Sermons of George Whitefield*, Watford: Church Society, 2010, vol. 1, p. 465.
25. Gatiss, *The Sermons of George Whitefield*, vol. 1, p. 416.
26. Gatiss, *The Sermons of George Whitefield*, vol. 1, p. 465.

27. Gatiss, *The Sermons of George Whitefield*, vol. 1, p. 395.

28. Noll, *The Rise of Evangelicalism*, p. 98.

29. Wesley and Whitefield clashed over the nature of the saving work of Christ upon the cross: is atonement available to all (Wesley) or only to the elect (Whitefield)?

30. W. Carus, *Charles Simeon, Memoir of the Life of the Rev. Charles Simeon*, London: J. Hatchard & Son, 1847, p. 703.

31. Jonathan Aitken, *John Newton*, London: Continuum, 2007, p. 180.

32. Hindmarsh, *The Evangelical Conversion Narrative*, p. 63.

33. Henry Rack, *Reasonable Enthusiast*, London: Epworth Press, 1989, p. 535.

34. Gatiss, *The Sermons of George Whitefield*, vol. 1, p. 13.

35. Noll, *The Rise of Evangelicalism*, p. 123.

3

Conversion and Call

Conversion lies at the heart of Evangelical identity.[1] The implications of conversion are not, however, merely to do with external distinctives but also with inward spirituality. Conversion not only marks out the Evangelical but also has a deep and profound impact upon Evangelical self-understanding and devotion. Evangelicals are converted people. Conversion affects the heart, the mind and indeed the whole person. Hence conversion for the Evangelical shapes both the calling into Christian service and the living of the Christian life. Evangelicals are characterized by radical transformation – "I once was lost, but now am found", wrote John Newton.[2]

For the Evangelical conversion also represents a story to be told. The experience provides a marker that the grace of God did indeed enter into the heart and mind of the believer in an identifiable way. The articulation of that transformation, and testimony concerning an individual's conversion, features strongly in Evangelical devotional life. Not only are Evangelicals converted, they both know that to be the case and can tell the story. The history of the various spiritual emphases within Evangelicalism illustrates some differences, but in essence conversion is a story received and a story to be retold (a story that changes one's own life as well as the lives of others). The sense of divine calling flows from conversion as an outward expression of the inward reality. Given the central place of assurance in Evangelical conversion, the idea of calling for the Evangelical is more objective than subjective. The conversion experience and the conversion narrative root that calling in the essential being of a Christian. This clearly locates the Evangelical call within the Protestant tradition of calling, with implications for the Christian life and for ministry and service.

Conversion

The archetypical conversion in Evangelical history was that of John Wesley. It was neither the only one, nor the first. The experience of Wesley in the meeting of a society of the Moravians in Aldersgate Street in the city of London in 1738 (see below) does, however, function as something of a model. It also illustrates that conversion, or more particularly, the story of conversion came into a particular prominence with the Revival in the first half of the eighteenth century. There are, of course, many famous examples of conversion in Christian history. Augustine in the fourth century and Luther in the sixteenth stand out as exemplars. However, in the case of other prominent Reformers – for example, John Calvin – although a conversion is asserted it is much harder to discern the story. In those instances the very narrative of being converted does not function in the same way in the life of the believer as it does from the eighteenth-century Revival onwards.

As the Evangelical Revival began to emerge in both Great Britain and North America, conversion featured prominently. Significant future leaders of the Revival were converted in the 1720s and 1730s, including Jonathan Edwards in North America, George Whitefield and both John and Charles Wesley. The conversion of the future leaders was followed by the conversion of future followers.

However, this conversion of the heart of the individual took place within a wider context. A number of distinctive trends were emerging which led to the Revival. One of these was the claim of the possibility of a personal encounter with God. Conversion was a feature of Puritan devotion but the emphasis upon personal encounter gave a new and particular emphasis to what became known as the "new birth". The conversion of August Francke in the period 1685–87[3] was the precursor to the growth of Pietist groups in, *inter alia*, Moravia, Bohemia and Silesia seeking to live out this encounter with God. As noted in Chapter 2, these communities stood in some continuity with earlier radical expressions of Protestantism.

In 1722 a community was established at Herrnhut on the estate of Count Nicholas von Zinzendorf. The emphasis was on personal piety and encounter with God. It was these Moravians who made contact with English Protestants in the 1730s, including John Wesley. The Wesleys, together with George Whitefield and others, were at this time seeking to deepen their own devotional life through the Holy Club in Oxford, reading classic works of devotion and holiness. Wesley was excited and intrigued by the Moravians' claim that they experienced personal encounter with God (he first met a group of them on a ship to the American colony of Georgia). The meeting of conversion and encounter proved to be powerful. The early Moravians still placed much weight upon the classic Puritan struggle with sin – from which conversion set them free. Later von Zinzendorf emphasized "stillness" and a devotion based on focusing one's gaze away from the self and upon the suffering Saviour.[4] We see here the beginnings of what later developed into rather different approaches to the Evangelical spiritual life – struggle or surrender. Ironically, what emerged in a corporate community setting was applied also in a much more individualist manner in the Revival. It was to a meeting of the Moravians that Wesley refers in his famous diary entry of 24 May 1738:

> *In the evening I went very unwillingly to a society in Aldersgate Street, where one was reading Luther's Preface to the Epistle to the Romans. About a quarter before nine, while he was describing the change which God works in the heart through faith in Christ, I felt my heart strangely warmed. I felt I did trust in Christ, Christ alone for salvation, and an assurance was given me that he had taken away my sins, even mine, and saved me from the law of sin and death.*[5]

There are four themes here: transformation of the heart, trust in Christ, assurance of salvation and personal rescue. The reference to describing the change which God wrought in the heart was neither new nor unusual, but the influence of Moravian piety is seen in the reference to the warming of the heart. In Evangelical devotion the change was being personalized. As we will see, it also became individualized. Wesley used the word "felt" twice in his description of his conversion. He introduced emotional feelings into the conversion narrative as an expression of relationship to God. Faith was to be "felt" as well as believed. However, this led to problems even for Wesley, when his feelings changed or subsided.

Trust in Christ was not just an affirmation of truth. It also reflected a genuine sense of dependence upon him alone for salvation, an important motif within Evangelical spirituality. This has been expressed in various ways, but particularly through the idea of God's daily providential care for the believer, which we will explore further in Chapter 4. The crux of the Evangelical concept of dependence and trust is that it is unmediated, a direct trust in and submission to Christ, with whom the believer is in a direct relationship.

Similarly important was the question of assurance. This concept is crucial to understanding Evangelical spirituality. The idea of assurance of salvation was not new in Protestant spirituality. Indeed, one of the significant spiritual contrasts with medieval Catholicism was that this assurance released the believer from the struggle to appease or satisfy God. Thus the Christian was set free also from dependency upon priests and ecclesiastical practices.

However, within Protestantism the struggle for acceptance with God was then replaced with a battle against sin in daily life. This remains an important element in Evangelical spirituality but the danger was a level of introspection that had the potential to turn the idea of assurance on its head. David Bebbington has pointed out that a change in the Evangelical understanding of assurance was one of the marks of the Revival.[6] This was as a direct result of the new Pietistic dependency upon God. Assurance of salvation released the believer from all struggle and was received in the heart by faith.

There were two problems.

First, as noted above, the introduction of "feelings" raised the question of what happens when feelings subside. John Wesley suffered significant turmoil in the days following his conversion. As Bruce Hindmarsh noted, "he was put into a quandary when his religious feeling ebbed."[7] Indeed, Wesley acknowledged that he had not experienced full assurance. From a scholarly perspective this also raises the question of how Wesley looked back in his second journal (written in 1740–42) on his 1738 experience – and indeed, the whole place of the Aldersgate Street experience in understanding Wesley.

Second, release from struggle against sin might lead to a more antinomian approach to the Christian life (that is, freedom from the ethical constraints of the law). Indeed, it did open up within Wesleyan Methodism the whole notion of Christian perfectionism and in the following century it developed into the holiness movement and the idea of "surrender" (see Chapter 5). Nevertheless, the doctrine of assurance came to a new prominence in the Evangelical spiritual life in the aftermath of the conversion of Wesley.

The fourth characteristic of the "model" Wesley conversion was that of personal rescue. The classic Protestant emphasis on being rescued through the atonement from sin, law and death is a key theme – the brand plucked from the fire. Wesley was described as such after being rescued as a child from a fire in his parents' rectory. The Evangelical convert was rescued also from the traditional heavy weight of medieval understandings of the law. This was an important corrective even to Wesley, who had been labouring within the Holy Club for a truly holy devotional life.

The Revival not only personalized conversion but also tended to individualize the experience. The Moravians encountered God in a personal way, but within community. Evangelical Pietists adopted the personal encounter with God, but perhaps, under the prevailing cultural influence of the Enlightenment, with its emphasis on the autonomy of the self, tended to understand the experience in very personal terms. Hence the experience of conversion was for the Evangelical deep, personal and individual. This not only illustrates Bebbington's wider theory of cultural influence upon Evangelicalism but also explains something of the nature and impact of Evangelical spirituality and devotion. This is part of the explanation for both the individualistic nature of much Evangelical piety and also the reason, as we will explore shortly, why so many individuals have arisen within the Evangelical tradition as exemplars and models of true piety. (This individualism may also explain why Evangelicals have so often found it hard to get along with each other.)

Charles Wesley experienced conversion three days before his brother: "I found myself convinced... I now found myself at peace with God, and rejoiced in hope of loving Christ."[8] Charles still struggled over the next few days but his faith was reinforced by John's experience. Charles had long wrestled with the idea that conversion was instantaneous and he fell out with John over the matter. Charles' own struggle was much affected by his frail health, in that dependence upon his own strength was not likely to succeed. He remarked that "I could not understand how this faith should be given in a moment."[9] After his own "warming of the heart" John shared with Charles that same evening his new-found assurance. Charles, despite his wavering since his own initial acceptance of Christ, responded that "at midnight I gave myself up to Christ; assured I was safe."[10] It was Susanna Wesley, full of enthusiasm, who reminded her son, "I do not judge it necessary for us to know the precise time of our conversion."[11]

George Whitefield (1714–70) was converted before either Wesley. He was part of John Wesley's Holy Club in Oxford where he had arrived at Pembroke College in 1732 in order to prepare for ordination. The path to ordination was a common one. Positively, it was viewed as a life of service. However, birth, opportunity, connections, status and even ambition played a part. Faith was not a prerequisite beyond the normal moralism of the times. Whitefield was converted in 1735 and then ordained in Gloucester Cathedral in 1736. Struggling with his quest for holiness, he described his longing for Christ and referred to being delivered from "the Burden that had so heavily oppressed me! The Spirit of Mourning was taken from me…" The response for Whitefield was to sing psalms of worship and he noted that "my Joy gradually became more settled, and, blessed be God, has abode and increased in my Soul (saving a few casual Intermissions) ever since."[12]

Converted people are often zealous and strong-willed. George Whitefield and John Wesley were both examples of such strength of character. No one at the time could have foreseen the significant impact that their ministries would have not only on the course of the Revival, but in the whole history of England. Many of the Revival leaders were Tories – the Countess of Huntingdon called the leadership to prayer when a French invasion seemed possible. For those committed to such radical methods, their adherence to order in society is perhaps slightly surprising. It certainly helped prevent revolution. Their stories are a potent reminder of how powerful a source of motivation the conversion narrative provides.

The story of John Newton is inspirational. He was born in 1725. His mother, Elizabeth, was a committed Christian, a member of a dissenting chapel in Wapping. His father, also John, with whom he had a tempestuous relationship, was a seafarer.

His mother died when he was seven years old. By the age of eleven he was at sea. The years that followed were characterized by the claims of love, the horrors of the press-gang, service in and desertion from the Navy, and a lifestyle increasingly at variance with his upbringing. He worked on a slave plantation in Africa, the experience being nothing short of a disaster, and he escaped by accepting the offer of a passage back to England on a trading ship, the *Greyhound*.

The year was 1748. The ship was not a slave-trader (that part of Newton's life came later) but it was here that he first encountered Christ. On board he read Thomas à Kempis' *The Imitation of Christ*. In his own words, he was "an infidel and libertine",[13] and it is not entirely clear why he should read anything remotely spiritual; it seems to have been simply boredom.[14] On 9 March 1748 he slammed the book shut with the thought, "what if these things should be true".[15]

He awoke in the early hours of 10 March to the anxious cries of the crew – the ship was sinking in what had begun as strong winds but was now a full Atlantic storm. The ship was battered and one man, together with all the livestock, was lost overboard. The crew were exhausted by the struggle for survival. Newton concluded a conversation with the captain with, "If this will not do, the Lord have mercy on us."[16] He himself later recalled, "I was instantly struck by my own words."[17] By 12 March, with the ship somewhat safer, Newton was recalling the promises of God which he had learned from Scripture as a youth.

As the ship emerged intact, Newton could see the hand of God at work and began to pray.

Newton, like Wesley, struggled a great deal after his conversion. He strayed. Indeed, his years as a captain of a slave-trader came after the momentous event on the *Greyhound*.

Newton did not, in retrospect, consider himself a true believer until some time after his conversion experience, although he always looked back on that day with great joy. He went on to become one of the leading Evangelical clergy in the Church of England, a vocal supporter of William Wilberforce and the anti-slavery movement, and through his hymnody and partnership with William Cowper, a significant contributor to Evangelical devotional piety.

Another individual who had long-term influence on the Established Church was Charles Simeon (1759–1836), who was first mentioned in Chapter 2. He arrived as an undergraduate at King's College, Cambridge in 1779 and had been in residence for just three days when he received a note from the Provost requiring attendance at Communion in three weeks' time. There was nothing unusual about this but, to put it mildly, Simeon viewed the prospect as a significant inconvenience. Once he had concluded that he could not avoid the obligation, Simeon went to the other extreme and decided he must prepare. His spiritual frenzy included fasting, study and prayer but it led only to an increased level of anxiety. He did not find the peace he sought in the sacrament. He knew that on Easter Day he must communicate again. He obtained as part of his devotional reading a book on the Lord's Supper by Bishop Wilson (1663–1755) and was struck by a particular reference which he summarized as: "the Jews knew what they did when they transferred their sin to the head of their offering."[18] Simeon continued in his own words:

> *The thought rushed into my mind, What! may I transfer all my guilt to another? Has God provided an offering for me, that I may lay my sins on his head? then, God willing, I will not bear them*

*on my own soul one moment longer. Accordingly
I sought to lay my sins upon the sacred head of
Jesus; and on the Wednesday began to have a hope
of mercy; on the Thursday that hope increased; on
the Friday and Saturday it became more strong;
and on the Sunday morning (Easter-day, April
4) I awoke early with these words upon my heart
and lips, "Jesus Christ is risen today! Hallelujah!
Hallelujah!" From that hour peace flowed in rich
abundance into my soul and at the Lord's Table in
our Chapel I had the sweetest access to God through
my blessed Saviour.*[19]

Conversion and the spiritual narrative and story which
flowed from it also reached into the ranks of the aristocracy
and indeed the clergy. Ordination then, as now, was not, in
Evangelical eyes, any guarantee of being converted.

The case of Selina, Countess of Huntingdon (who was
born in 1707 and died the same year as John Wesley, 1791),
is interesting because her conversion, in mid 1739, was not at
all like that of Wesley. Even more so since the Countess was
one of the key leaders of the Revival in the middle decades of
the eighteenth century. As well as acting as a conduit for the
gospel into the English aristocracy, she also remained close
friends with both Wesley and Whitefield. She established
chapels and appointed chaplains which eventually, towards
the end of the century, found expression in the Countess
of Huntingdon's Connexion. Selina herself did not point
to a specific conversion experience. However, there is no
doubt that such an experience took place. We know that
she was converted through the witness of her sister-in-law,
Lady Margaret Hastings, who was linked to Whitefield and

married one of Wesley's colleagues, Benjamin Ingham. We also have some extracts from letters. In 1766 she referred to prayer over twenty-seven years (hence 1739) and in July 1739 her sister-in-law Margaret referred to the good work the Lord had done in Selina. The Countess herself told her half-sister, Lady Betty, "I feel every day there is no delight and pleasure in this world equal to the convictions of pious souls. It raises the heart so much above all earthly things."[20]

Although she did not have an Aldersgate Street experience to record or articulate, the Countess was able to point to a period of religious intensity, seriousness and searching, out of which she emerged as a committed Evangelical. Others have followed this path also (including both Wilberforce and Shaftesbury) and it reflects more the experience of some of the Reformers. So conversion is central to Evangelical piety but the experience is not identical for all and not in every instance the sudden heart-warming experience of the Wesleyan model.

William Haslam

William Haslam (1818–1905) is of interest as the clergyman converted by his own sermon in 1851. As the Rector of Baldhu, near Truro, in the Diocese of Exeter, Haslam struggled with the whole concept of salvation. He sought advice from a neighbouring Evangelical cleric, Robert Aitken, who questioned whether Haslam had grasped justification by faith and recommended he told his congregation that he would not preach to them again until he was converted. That is what he planned to do on one particular Sunday. The story is so extraordinary and illustrative (bearing in mind, of course, the limits of later self-testimony) that we should allow Haslam to recount it in his own words:

And while I was reading the Gospel, I thought, well, I will just say a few words in explanation of this, and then I will dismiss them. So I went up into the pulpit and gave out my text. I took it from the gospel of the day — "What think ye of Christ?" (Matt. xxii. 42).

As I went on to explain the passage, I saw that the Pharisees and scribes did not know that Christ was the Son of God, or that He was come to save them. They were looking for a king, the son of David, to reign over them as they were. Something was telling me all the time, "You are no better than the Pharisees yourself — you do not believe that He is the Son of God, and that He is come to save you, any more than they did." I do not remember all I said, but I felt a wonderful light and joy coming into my soul, and I was beginning to see what the Pharisees did not. Whether it was something in my words, or my manner, or my look, I know not but all of a sudden a local preacher, who happened to be in the congregation, stood up, and putting up his arms, shouted out in Cornish manner, "The parson is converted! the parson is converted! Hallelujah!" and in another moment his voice was lost in the shouts and praises of three or four hundred of the congregation. Instead of rebuking this extraordinary "brawling", as I should have done in a former time, I joined in the outburst of praise and to make it more orderly, I gave out the Doxology — Praise God, from whom all blessings flow — and the people sang it with heart and voice, over and over again. My Churchmen were dismayed, and many of them

*fled precipitately from the place. Still the voice
of praise went on, and was swelled by numbers
of passers-by, who came into the church, greatly
surprised to hear and see what was going on.*

*When this subsided, I found at least twenty
people crying for mercy, whose voices had not been
heard in the excitement and noise of thanksgiving.
They all professed to find peace and joy in believing.
Amongst this number there were three from my own
house and we returned home praising God.*

*The news spread in all directions that "the
parson was converted", and that by his own
sermon, in his own pulpit! The church would
not hold the crowds who came in the evening. I
cannot exactly remember what I preached about
on that occasion but one thing I said was, "that
if I had died last week I should have been lost for
ever." I felt it was true. So clear and vivid was
the conviction through which I had passed, and
so distinct was the light into which the Lord had
brought me, that I knew and was sure that He
had "brought me up out of an horrible pit, out
of the miry clay, and set my feet upon a Rock,
and put a new song into my mouth" (Ps. xl.). He
had "quickened" me, who was before "dead in
trespasses and sins" (Eph. ii. 1).*[21]

The reaction of those referred to by Haslam as "my
churchmen" shows the often negative reaction of others to
Evangelical conversion. The experience of rejection and
opposition was a common one from the time of the Revival
onwards.

The leaders of the Revival provided models for others to follow.[22] In this way conversion became a key theme of the Evangelical spiritual tradition. Bruce Hindmarsh[23] has noted how Evangelicals came to record their conversion narratives in journals and other media so that the story of conversion came to form a crucial aspect of Evangelical self-understanding. The story also formed part of Evangelical devotion since personal accounts of conversion were popular testimonies in the congregational setting. So Evangelical individualism was located once again in a more corporate context.

Story and testimony link the experience of conversion to Evangelical devotional practice. The ability to articulate the journey to faith is characteristic of Evangelicalism. For some this will be an experience as specific as that of John Wesley. For others the conversion experience will be more nebulous, like Calvin, the Countess of Huntingdon, William Wilberforce and the Earl of Shaftesbury, but like them, they will be able to tell a story of "before" and "after", of deepening intensity and of the work of grace in the heart. The congregational gathering forms a crucial place for this articulation. Indeed, the early Methodist "band" meetings functioned in this way. Hence contemporary Evangelicalism is likely to place some weight in its devotional practice on congregational testimony. There is a story to be told. That narrative forms part not only of the heritage of the individual but also of the wider Evangelical tradition of which that individual is part, consciously or otherwise.

The conversion narrative also functions as inspiration. The stories and testimonies of the historic heroes of the faith act as models, exemplars and motivators in the life of discipleship. This is often reflected in a desire to know more of the history of the tradition, the practice of reading biography, learning from the strengths and weaknesses of those who have gone before, and a desire to replicate the spiritual intensity and activism which they represent. Sometimes this can be problematic, as attempts to imitate can fail to take account of changed context. Ironically, Evangelicalism has been both the instigator of some of the most radical approaches to Christian life and mission and, at the same time, the originator of traditions which rather too quickly become invested with apostolic status.

So conversion is central. It models, it inspires and leads to a greater intensity of devotional practice in prayer and in attention to Scripture. It is the basis of our call to Christian life and witness, and indeed to evangelism. Devotional practices which are determined by this narrative may include oral testimony, the keeping of a journal, writing down one's own conversion story and prayer for the conversion of others. The context of conversion may vary but the actual experience can be broad enough to encompass a variety of events and happenings. The impact, however, is unchanging down the centuries, leading to new birth, to a new spiritual heart and to a renewed understanding of the call to be a Christian.

To the impact of conversion on an individual's sense of call we now turn.

Calling

Evangelicals have a deep sense of spiritual calling. However, this call, or vocation, has a number of specific characteristics that distinguish Evangelical piety. Many of these features have become somewhat obscured. In essence the call of an

Evangelical flows out from the conversion experience. Indeed, it is this combination that often leads to the activism that is acknowledged as a distinguishing feature of the Evangelical tradition.

The first and most important aspect to understanding the nature of calling, for the Evangelical, is to place it firmly within the historic Protestant tradition. Martin Luther, in his *Address to the Christian Nobility of the German Nation*, made the points powerfully. It is, he said, "pure invention that pope, bishops, priests and monks are to be called the 'spiritual estate'; princes, lords, artisans, and farmers the 'temporal estate'." Rather, he went on, "all Christians are truly of the 'spiritual estate', and there is among them no difference at all but that of office." Luther related this essential calling to baptism, the call to royal priesthood as set out in 1 Peter 2:9 and the call to be priests and kings in Revelation 5:10. He summarized the position:

> *A cobbler, a smith, a farmer, each has the work and office of his trade, and yet they are all alike consecrated priests and bishops, and every one by means of his own work or office must benefit and serve every other, that in this way many kinds of work may be done for the bodily and spiritual welfare of the community, even as all the members of the body serve one another.*[24]

John Wycliffe (1324–84) had previously articulated this understanding. Naturally, in the history of Christianity, this position has sometimes been misapplied within the Protestant tradition to mean that there is no distinctive calling to be a minister. However, the distortion has usually arisen in the

other direction with an overemphasis on the special nature of
the calling to ministry and priesthood, sometimes set against
the wider call. Evangelicals too have been affected with a
tendency to place too much weight upon calling either to
ordained ministry or perhaps to the mission field.

Important as these callings are, it is essential to deal with
first principles. Evangelicals will want to relate Christian
calling to conversion rather than baptism (though in Luther's
context that link is understandable, and, of course, the convert
should be baptized), and assert that the life of devotional
Christian service is equally applicable to the entire range of
life's occupations and business. This will have a profound
impact upon the spiritual life of the believer. Even when
the understanding of call within Evangelical congregational
life is widened, it is often only to the caring professions.
The Christian convert may have a deep calling to life as an
architect, a business career, a political career as well as to
nursing, teaching and ordained and missionary offices.

The spiritual implications are very deep. The Christian
will wish to nurture their call, to understand their role in
business, in community and in society as a call from God
and an expression of their Christian service. They will wish
to develop an understanding of that call as vocational, from
God. This can be transformative for both the individual
and the church. The individual is nurtured in their call and
service for the Lord, rather than, as Christians in business
are sometimes made to feel, treated as second class, and the
congregation of the Lord's people are encouraged to pray for
and nurture all of its members in their calling.

However, understanding this basic biblical idea of calling
also equips the Christian convert better for the Christian life,
not least in the management of stress, in giving priority to

family and in respecting life's boundaries. Frequently, those called into full-time ordained Christian work ask how they are to avoid burn-out. The fact that this question is even asked demonstrates the importance, for the Evangelical spiritual life, of understanding the call of all the Lord's people.

If ordained Christian ministry is viewed as something separate and special in essence from other roles in life, then two things flow. First, the individual will suffer from the demand to be available at all times and not be able to plan family time and boundaries effectively. Second, all others may feel unaffirmed and second-class citizens. However, once it is recognized that the call to ordained ministry is at one with the call to business, caring and other roles, offices and occupations, then it is realized that the ordained Christian worker, like everybody else, has to manage life's responsibilities and boundaries in a way that honours God, family and work.

Before turning to some examples, we need to ask how this call manifests itself within the Evangelical tradition. In short, for the Evangelical the call will be active, objective and individual. As we will see, this carries with it both strengths and weaknesses. Evangelicals are called to do something! Although Evangelical spirituality should not be seen as excluding contemplation, study and prayer, the essence of the call is to action. Clearly, the Evangelical tradition would do well to learn the relationship of the outward and the inward (that is, prayer sustains action), but given the foundational role of conversion, the inward heart has already been transformed and call is a function of that conversion.

Hence the call will not only be active, but also objective. Evangelicals will often struggle with vague notions of vocation developing subjectively and needing some additional external objective affirmation. Evangelicals will have a heightened sense of God's call upon their life as a direct consequence of their conversion. Thus the call will also very often be individual much more than corporate. These characteristics carry the advantages of a personal, specific, active and objective spiritual understanding of call for Evangelicals. This understanding has led to great things being done by men and women of God. Similarly, it has meant that significant numbers of Christian people are motivated and empowered because they are responding to God's call upon their lives. We will see all of this modelled shortly in some examples. However, we also need to recognize the weaknesses of the classic Evangelical model and ask whether the various influences upon the Evangelical spiritual tradition might offer some nuances.

The main weaknesses which Evangelicalism suffers from in respect of calling are individualism, lack of sustainability and an ambiguous attitude to prayer. We have already shown how individualism brings great strengths to the tradition. However, one consequence of a considerable number of people experiencing a significant call on their lives is that it can lead to such diversity that it contributes to the fragmentation of Evangelicalism, with its numerous societies, missions, leaders, pastors, churches and so on.

A second area of concern is that the individual, objective and active nature of call for the Evangelical can lead to an excessively short-term approach to life, ministry and faith. If the call does not lead to immediate success (after all, it is God who has called), then this leads to despair or disillusionment. Evangelicals need to relearn the importance of sustaining call for the long term.

Third, we Evangelicals need to be honest about our

ambiguous attitude towards prayer. Many of the great Christian leaders of history were prayer warriors. Today, and linked to the point about lack of sustainability, there has been something of a loss, within the Evangelical spiritual tradition, of sustained prayer. The fear of overemphasis on any subjective or inner vocation or call has sometimes meant that there has not been that long-term commitment to nurturing call through prayer.

The classic Reformed or Puritan influence upon Evangelicalism tends to emphasize the objective and active nature of call. The renewed influence of Pietism and the personal encounter with God means increasing weight is given to the subjective and individual nature of the call. One of the other long-term strands of Evangelical spirituality has been the "holiness" tradition. This history, as noted in Chapter 1, can be traced from aspects of Pietism, through what was known as the holiness movement in the nineteenth century, and also features in some aspects of modern Pentecostal and Charismatic spiritual traditions. The holiness tradition, like all others, carries strengths and weaknesses. However, in respect of call, one of the positive influences of the historic holiness movement is that it gives some greater weight to the inward, subjective relationship to God. In more contemporary terminology, the notion of "waiting" upon the Lord gives expression to this. We should harness the strengths of this approach as an appropriate balance to the more usual objective, active and individual approach to call, encouraging prayer and sustainability, without losing sight of the objective reality of the call of God upon the lives of believers.

Evangelical history is full of giants. These were usually humble men and women used greatly by God. Two great leaders in the eighteenth and nineteenth centuries, both from families of considerable social standing, were William Wilberforce and Anthony Ashley Cooper, the seventh Earl of Shaftesbury. They both experienced the clear call of God to serve him in politics, in the public square. After reviewing their stories we will look also at a more traditional Evangelical story – a missionary call, in this case to C. T. Studd, in the latter part of the nineteenth century.

Wilberforce, born in Hull in 1759, was greatly influenced by a family friend, one of Yorkshire's Evangelical pioneers, Isaac Milner. He also came under the influence of his devout aunt and uncle. He was a seeker. He read Philip Doddridge's *The Rise and Progress of Religion in the Soul*. With Milner, who carried with him a Greek New Testament, Wilberforce travelled across Europe over a period of several months, beginning in 1784. Through their conversations Wilberforce became intellectually convinced of the claims of Christ, but was not yet persuaded in his heart.

In the autumn of 1785 Wilberforce underwent a conversion. Unlike Wesley, Wilberforce could not point to a single moment of conversion, but similar to Wesley, he struggled with self-doubt afterwards. The question he faced was what he should do about his fledgling public political career in the light of this conversion. It is clear that Wilberforce considered very seriously indeed withdrawing from public life. This prompted a response from Prime Minister Pitt. As Wilberforce's recent biographer put it, "Pitt's plea to Wilberforce that a Christian life should produce action rather than mere meditation was well considered, and may have made its mark."[25]

After further agonizing, Wilberforce delivered a letter to John Newton, then Rector of St Mary, Woolnoth in the City of London, on 4 December 1785, requesting a meeting.

Newton offered wise counsel to Wilberforce and fortified him in recognizing that his Christian call was to politics rather than to ordination. Newton fully understood that an Evangelical Parliamentarian would face many pressures,[26] writing to Cowper in 1786, that Wilberforce was not on the right track in thinking of ordination, but that he had considerable abilities and ample scope for usefulness in public life. Newton added, "I hope the Lord will make him a blessing both as a Christian and a statesman..."[27] In 1796 he told Wilberforce:

> *I believe you are the Lord's servant, and are in the post which He has assigned you; and though it appears to me more arduous, and requiring more self-denial than my own, I know that He who has called you to it can afford you strength according to your day.*[28]

The nation was to be thankful that Wilberforce found his call. One of the distinctive features in Wilberforce's life was the wise counsel of others, notably experienced Christians. This is an aspect of vocation and call which has sometimes been neglected by Evangelicals.

The full, inspiring story of the seventh Earl of Shaftesbury can be found in his most recent biography.[29] Lord Ashley, as he was known prior to his accession to the Earldom in 1851, is a classic example of an Evangelical call to public life and service. For a young aristocrat in his position, a career in politics was the normal path to take. The difference with Shaftesbury was that his entry into public service was founded in his Evangelical conversion and call from God to serve.[30] In October 1825, Ashley, looking to the forthcoming election, in which he was a candidate for the first time, in the Tory interest at Woodstock, wrote in his diary, "I have a great mind to found a policy upon the Bible."[31] There are clear signs in this period that Ashley was going beyond the traditional positions of a Tory aristocrat. He was quickly appointed to a minor office in government. All of this came together in the clear call of God on Ashley's life, an essential prerequisite to a life of Christian service. In 1827 he had written in his diary: "I desire to be useful in my generation, and die in the knowledge of having advanced happiness by having advanced true religion."[32] He had earlier declared: "I want nothing but usefulness to God and my country."[33] His mood oscillated between his self-deprecation at his lack of fitness for service and his increasing sense of call:

> *Every one chooses his career and it is well if he chooses that which is best suited to his talents. I have taken political life because I have, by God's blessing, many advantages of birth and situation which, although of trifling value if unsupported, are yet very powerful aids if joined to zeal and honesty. It is here, therefore, that I have the chief way of being useful to my generation.*[34]

Shaftesbury thus illustrates some important aspects of vocation and call for the Evangelical. The call to Shaftesbury was objective, individual and active – a desire for usefulness in public and political service. Although the more subjective elements of call are not so obviously present in Shaftesbury, prayer, self-examination and indeed an inner struggle did feature. There was a dependency on God and a desire to serve him in the gospel in the public square.

Turning to an example of call to Christian missionary

service, the story of C. T. Studd and the Cambridge Seven who sailed for China in February 1885 is a marvellous record of the work of God. His call is also illustrative and shows the influence of the holiness movement and a holistic and integrated approach. Studd was a cricketer who played for England alongside W. G. Grace and captained the Cambridge University side. He was converted under the ministry of the American evangelist D. L. Moody (see Chapter 7). After this experience Studd noted that he "wanted to win souls for the Lord"[35] and desired to know what his life's work would be. He recorded that he then spent some three months in prayer and Bible reading (a helpful corrective for Evangelicalism's sometimes over-emphasized immediacy in call), still without clarity. Under the influence of the holiness movement and Moody, whose theology was closely aligned to it, Studd then came to a position where he stated: "I had kept myself from him, and had not wholly yielded." His response was that he "gave myself up to God", singing Frances Ridley Havergal's hymn, "Take my life and let it be, consecrated, Lord to thee".[36] His passion for souls led to the call to China. The theme of surrender or yielding, so characteristic of the nineteenth-century holiness movement, was deeply influential upon later Evangelicalism's understanding of call. It enables contemporary Evangelicalism to have a more creative interaction between objective and subjective elements of the call of God upon the life of the believer.

How then does Evangelical spirituality understand the call to ordained ministry? Essentially in the same way as any other call. In other words, it is an objective, individual call to service predicated upon conversion. Evangelicals are less likely to be able to articulate an "inner journey", though as we have seen, genuine struggle with prayer and Scripture is an integral part of all Evangelical spirituality.

How can we summarize the spirituality of vocation and call for the Evangelical? We have seen at different times and in various examples the different balances of the objective and the subjective. The objective clarity of the call from God to serve him did not prevent spiritual struggle; indeed, a period of sustained Scripture reading and prayer was a reminder of the importance of the basic spiritual disciplines. For the Evangelical, though, the call is always active; it is a call to usefulness, faithfulness and service in the work of God. Crucially, this call is for all, and ordination, missionary work, or other forms of paid Christian employment, are simply one aspect of call among many. The call is individual, empowered by the experience of conversion. The individuality of the call carries the strength of conviction and the weakness of excessive diversity, leading sometimes to duplication and lack of coherence in Christian work.

In contemporary Evangelical spirituality the individuality of the call is also sometimes internalized, especially among some of those most influenced by Charismatic spirituality with its roots in the holiness and revivalist movements. The effect of this can be to overemphasize the subjective at the expense of the objective. This is a call from God, to me, in my heart. Evangelical spirituality has lost much of its sense of history and we would be helped a great deal by recovering some of the insights of those who have gone before. There is much to celebrate in the universality of call, its active ingredient of Christian service and the power of its individual nature. History reminds us that the wise counsel of other Christians is important and the internal spiritual disciplines of prayer and Scripture are bedrocks. The key to understanding call in Evangelical spirituality is to recognize that it flows essentially from the conversion experience. That is what gives call its powerful effect; the converted Christian experiences God's call into Christian service in the world.

Notes

1. David Bebbington, *Evangelicalism in Modern Britain*, London: Unwin Hyman, 1989, pp. 5–10; Richard Turnbull, *Anglican and Evangelical?*, London: Continuum, 2007 (reprinted 2010), pp. 55–62.
2. *Olney Hymnbook*, London, 1779, facsimile copy of the original, Cowper and Newton Museum, Olney, 1979.
3. D. Bruce Hindmarsh, *The Evangelical Conversion Narrative*, Oxford: OUP, 2005, p. 58.
4. Hindmarsh, *Evangelical Conversion Narrative*, p. 164.
5. Wesley, *Works*, quoted in Hindmarsh, *Evangelical Conversion Narrative*, p. 121.
6. Bebbington, *Evangelicalism in Modern Britain*, pp. 42–50.
7. Hindmarsh, *Evangelical Conversion Narrative*, p. 121.
8. *Journal of Revd Charles Wesley*, i, 90, quoted in Gary Best, *Charles Wesley*, Peterborough: Epworth, 2006, p. 92.
9. Wesley, *Works*, i, 91, quoted in Best, *Charles Wesley*, p. 88.
10. *Journal of Revd Charles Wesley*, i, 95, quoted in Best, *Charles Wesley*, p. 93.
11. Best, *Charles Wesley*, p. 94.
12. *Journal of George Whitefield*, quoted in Hindmarsh, *Evangelical Conversion Narrative*, p. 107.
13. Newton Memorial, inscribed on tombstone in Olney churchyard, quoted by Jonathan Aitken, *John Newton*, London: Continuum, 2007, p. 356.
14. Aitken, *Newton*, p. 72.
15. Aitken, *Newton*, p. 73.
16. Aitken, *Newton*, p. 76.
17. Aitken, *Newton*, p. 76.
18. Michael Hennell and Arthur Pollard (eds), *Charles Simeon (1759–1836)*, London: SPCK, 1959, p. 24.
19. Hennel and Pollard, *Charles Simeon*, pp. 24–25.
20. Faith Cook, *Selina, Countess of Huntingdon*, Edinburgh: Banner of Truth Trust, 2001, pp. 36–37.

21. William Haslam, *From Death to Life*, Darlington: Evangelical Press, 2004.

22. For other examples of conversion in the Revival see Richard Turnbull, *Reviving the Heart: The Story of the Eighteenth Century Revival*, Oxford: Lion, 2012.

23. Hindmarsh, *Evangelical Conversion Narrative*, p. 92.

24. Martin Luther, "An Open Letter to the Christian Nobility of the German Nation" in Luther, *Works*, Philadelphia: Muhlenberg Press, 1943, Volume 2, page 69.

25. William Hague, *William Wilberforce*, London: Harper Perennial, 2008, p. 87. See also Aitken, *Newton*, p. 301.

26. Aitken, *Newton*, p. 302.

27. Aitken, *Newton*, p. 304.

28. Hague, *Wilberforce*, p. 88.

29. Richard Turnbull, *Shaftesbury: The Great Reformer*, Oxford: Lion, 2010.

30. Turnbull, *Shaftesbury*, chapters two and three.

31. Lord Ashley, *Diaries*, 13 October 1825, Turnbull, *Shaftesbury*, p. 21.

32. Lord Ashley, *Diaries*, 22 April 1827, Turnbull, *Shaftesbury*, p. 24.

33. Lord Ashley, *Diaries*, 22 February 1827, Turnbull, *Shaftesbury*, p. 24.

34. Turnbull, *Shaftesbury*, p. 28.

35. Norman Grubb, *C. T. Studd*, London: Religious Tract Society, 1933, p. 34.

36. Grubb, *Studd*, p. 38.

4

Providence and Prayer

....

J ohn Calvin (1509–64) was the great theologian of
the sovereignty of God. According to Calvin, the
inevitable consequence of the nature of God and his
sovereignty was that humanity was not "whirled and twisted
about by blindly indiscriminate fortune, rather than governed
by God's providence."[1] In his journal William Wilberforce
reflected upon his providential encounter with Isaac Milner,
his coming across Doddridge's *Rise and Progress*, and his own
protection from evil and danger, all crucial elements of his
call, which we considered in Chapter 3.[2] At various times the
hand of God has been perceived also in financial crisis, in
political and moral campaigns, in missionary expeditions and
indeed in the creation of the British Empire or other nation
states. Miracles, healings, supernatural gifts and instances of
guidance, past and present, may also be seen as examples of
God's sovereignty, displaying the rich, yet complex, mosaic
of the nature of God's providence in Christian discipleship.

The direct action of God in the life of the individual
believer is a key characteristic of Evangelical devotion and
piety. In one sense, given the centrality of conversion, this is
not at all surprising. However, the idea of God's *providence* is
primarily to do with the overall way in which God shapes,
plans, guides and intervenes in the life of the Christian
disciple. The concept of providence also extends further than

the individual believer to include God's care of and purposes for society and the universe generally. We are concerned with the nature of God and his actions. Hence, in terms of the spiritual life, we need to consider the extent to which God works through the existing order and the nature of any miraculous intervention.

The matter of prayer is crucial. All Christians believe in prayer, but what difference does it make? Is it possible to influence the actions of God through prayer? The relationship between providence and prayer prompts us to reflect again upon the different ways in which the various sources, traditions and influences of Evangelical theology and spirituality express themselves, both historically and in contemporary devotion. So, for example, the prayer that leads to a provision of a parking space and the prayer for healing of an ailment may both involve miracle, and both have to face up to serious questions concerning the interventionist nature of God in the face of Auschwitz or the Gulag. Evangelical Christians, however, have always been willing to pray for matters of nature (the weather), the world (peace and oppression), medical and financial need and practical daily living. Our concern is to understand both why and how God responds and works through such prayer. In outline, given the background spiritual traditions we have considered, those most influenced by the Calvinist or Reformed traditions will give the greatest weight to God working through the natural order, with prayer understood as aligning the heart with God's will. On the other hand, the revivalist traditions will emphasize more of the miraculous intervention of God brought about by the fervent prayers of the believer. The entire range of the Evangelical tradition believes in prayer and intervention. The differences arise over the manner and nature of God's providence and the consequent place of prayer – which leads to some variances in spiritual practices.

To what extent does God work through the natural order? As with most Christians, Evangelicals believe in a God of order, and this belief begins with the divine ordering of the Trinity. The majesty and sovereignty of God flow from this, including his providential actions. Calvin is an important starting point for our discussion, because the *Institutes of the Christian Religion* not only contain an extensive reflection upon the natural order but have also deeply informed the mainstream of Reformed Christian thinking ever since. Although there is scholarly debate over the extent to which he allowed for natural theology, Calvin saw God's glory manifest in the "distinct and well-ordered variety of the heavenly host".[3] He also clearly refers to the implanting of clear and prominent marks (pointers to the nature of God) in the universe so that no one could make pleas of ignorance.

The problem in discerning Reformed and Evangelical views on natural theology is the weight which is given to sin in obscuring the natural order. The consequence of sin in the natural world is that God's purposes in creation are marred and concealed. Hence, depending on the emphasis given, it is not possible to apprehend God in the natural order at all or, at best, it is not possible to know him fully. Only with the benefits of the revelation of God in Christ can God the Creator be apprehended in the natural universe.

The continuing character of divine providence was essential to Calvin: "we see the presence of divine power shining as much in the continuing state of the universe as in its conception." God was not only the Creator, but also "everlasting Governor and Preserver",[4] not only establishing the framework but also sustaining, nourishing and caring for it. This lies at the heart of the debate about divine providence – the relationship between God as Creator and sustainer and the nature of his continued involvement. Calvin gave the example of the sun. The sun provides light and heat, but God could dispense with the need for the instrument of the sun and act himself directly, if he so wishes – as in Joshua 10:13, when the sun stood still for two days, and Isaiah 38:8, when its shadow went back by ten degrees. Calvin wrote: "God has witnessed by those few miracles that the sun does not daily rise and set by a blind instinct of nature but that he himself, to renew our remembrance of his fatherly favour toward us, governs its course."[5] He added: "providence means not that by which God idly observes from heaven what takes place on earth, but that by which, as keeper of the keys, he governs all events."[6]

Hence we begin to see in Calvin that there are three issues in respect of providence. First, there are God's general actions through the natural order – the laws of nature, climate and science. Second, there is the question of particular interventions by God – which might be referred to as miracles. Third, there is the matter of the ongoing relationship of God to the created order, including humanity. Calvin is a fine example of how general and particular providence come together in a way that has distinguished Reformed and Evangelical teaching.

By the time of the Evangelical Revival there had been a considerable change in the intellectual and cultural climate, through what is known as the Enlightenment. Christian thinkers began to adapt their understanding of order and the universe in the light of reason and rationality. Take the example of William Paley (1743–1805). In his *Natural Theology*

Paley used examples such as the eye and the workings of a watch to illustrate his argument that particular purposes were achieved through general laws via, for example, the apparatus of an eye rather than by the creation of a new law or the suspension of an old law. This broader framework of "orthodox" thinking clearly influenced Evangelical thought. For some, this developed into the "iron laws of Ricardian political economy",[7] or Adam Smith's "invisible hand" – although for most Evangelicals, the prevalence of sin at least acted as something of a constraint on political economy. Roger Anstey has linked this thinking to Evangelicalism by noting the caution shown in detecting interference with the regular course of nature, and Wilberforce referred his readers to Joseph Butler's *Analogy of Religion*, a work very much in accord with that of Paley. Evangelicals stood within the tradition of much Enlightenment thinking in respect of order and providence. Indeed, this is one aspect of David Bebbington's[8] wider thesis on the influence upon Evangelicalism of the prevailing patterns of cultural thought. The concentration on order also gave weight to the idea of dividing history into dispensations, as discussed in Chapter 2.

However, despite this caution, Evangelical societies, newspapers and individuals all clearly associated providence with specific contemporary and historical events.[9] In this they were quite different from Paley and Butler and, following Calvin, reflected the Evangelical concern to maintain a more direct involvement of God in his world, rather than to view him merely as a remote designer. Conversion was, as we have seen, essential to the Evangelical scheme, and there could surely be no more certain instance of God's continuing action and intervention than in an Evangelical conversion.

The early Evangelicals looked back to Calvin but

clearly extended the thinking somewhat further, which opened the way for later developments. These Evangelical pioneers wished to maintain the principle of divine order while retaining a place for the direct action of God. God's sovereignty meant that he did not need to disclose the reasons for his providential actions.[10] God's sovereignty also reigned in an unfathomable way over election and, importantly for the next generation of Evangelicals, the conversion of the Jews before the end of time.

These ideas of order and harmony were significant for the Evangelical understanding of God and his universe and of his action in the world. To the Evangelical, the God of order could only create a systematic cosmos. Hence there was an Evangelical natural theology which saw the harmony of God in the regularity and measure of the created world. It is an important element of Evangelical spiritual devotion to recognize the distinctive work of God as Creator as well as Redeemer. In contemporary debates on environmental concerns this heritage is of some importance – it is the impact of sin upon God's creation, Evangelicals contend, which threatens the natural order.

A further example comes from the discussions at the Eclectic Society on 11 November 1811. The topic for enquiry was the appearance of Halley's Comet. Josiah Pratt expressed the common understanding: "It may rouse us to the recollection that the government of God is proceeding on determined laws, how much soever may be hid from our observation."[11] Hence the comet illustrated God's unlimited power and humbled human beings in their ignorance. The future Bishop of Calcutta, Daniel Wilson, emphasized the concept of order when he stated that "heavenly bodies are employed, particularly in Scripture, to demonstrate the stability of the covenant God makes with his people."[12] Cosmic order was invested with divine significance for both society and the church.

So Evangelicals, like their spiritual forebears, believed in order. Sometimes this was expressed in a conservatism that rather belied the radical nature of many of the movement's key concerns and emphases. Inevitably there was also a more radical edge to the Reformed heritage which expressed something of a different view. We see this from the Anabaptists to the Puritan radicals under Cromwell ("the Levellers"). This more radical element was carried forward into the Evangelical Revival by the Quakers and the inner light traditions. This background can help explain some of the modern radical Evangelical movements.

Evangelicals in the Church of England were particularly attracted to order through the idea of "establishment", a view that gained ground especially in the aftermath of the French Revolution in 1789, when Evangelicals as much as any others pleaded the cause of peace and harmony in an ordered society. Wilberforce's conservatism came out in his claim that the Supreme Being had so arranged "the constitution of things, as to render the prevalence of true Religion and of pure morality conducive to the well-being of states, and the preservation of civil order."[13] Hence the purpose of an Established Church was to encourage godliness (and resist ungodliness) and to promote right religion and the fear of God in the nation. The establishment principle was seen as having great weight in campaigns for public morality and, for example, against the secularization of the Sabbath. The issue of establishment explains something of the rather uneasy tension between Evangelicals within the Established Church, and dissenters belonging to the free churches. There was a natural spiritual sympathy, but nevertheless individuals such as Simeon and, indeed, the Wesleys expressed a quite stringent adherence to establishment and order within the church. Others were more eclectic, including the Earl of Shaftesbury.

In the light of this heritage and the various cultural influences, how then did Evangelicals view the nature of God's providence and intervention? Following Calvin, the early Evangelicals drew a distinction between "general providence" and "particular (or special) providence".

General providence referred to God's action in the universe through natural law and cause and effect. A belief in general providence did not exclude miracle, as we will see, but this form of providence was indirect. General providence was exercised through second causes – for example, God determined the laws of nature which governed the weather which in turn produced a hurricane. Hence the hurricane is within the providence of God. Josiah Pratt, at the Eclectic Society, defined general providence as "the government of the world by that influence of second causes which God has connected with them".

But when God acted directly through a primary cause, this direct – perhaps miraculous – intervention amounted to *special* or *particular* providence, that is, "an effect produced by the appointment of God". According to Pratt, special providence involved only those effects which were either contrary to natural causes, above natural causes or as a result of some extraordinary combination of natural causes. Hence, although this allowed for miracle, in very many cases special providence was not to be distinguished from general, and what appeared to be particular was often "the common cause of general providence".[14]

Pratt was displaying the typical reserve of the early Evangelicals in discerning acts of special providence. Since the laws of the universe reflected God's ordering, then it was generally through those laws that God worked. Pratt's advice to those who claimed to see special providential actions of God was to exercise caution, even suspicion. The suggestion of special intervention was to be rejected if it was contrary to the Word, and accepted only when the tendency was to sanctify – in other words, the test for the veracity of the special intervention was whether there was demonstrable spiritual fruit and growth consistent with Scripture. He stressed that as much gratitude was owed for the operation of the usual course of events as for the turning aside of that course, and that special providences were too often made to serve a particular purpose.

Other commentators at the discussions of the Eclectic Society concurred, warning against too hasty a conclusion from events. John Newton added that there was no such thing as an accident. All of this clearly aligns the Evangelical mainstream with the moderate view of Calvinist determinism. However, it is also clear that Evangelicals wished to find some place for a more directly interventionist view of God.

The use of national days of prayer and fasting in the nineteenth century was one example of the early Evangelicals giving more weight to particular providence. So too was their attitude to other national and international events. In 1803 one commentator in an Eclectic Society discussion saw Napoleon Bonaparte as God's instrument. In 1808 another saw God's wrath as descending upon the nation due to sins sanctioned by statute, oppression in the colonies, the profaning of the Sabbath and the existence of gin shops and lotteries. In 1811, John Clayton stated, "[that] God has a controversy with this nation is too evident to be doubted",[15] and another speaker remarked, "it is evident that God's judgements are abroad in the earth".[16] Hence something of the tension in Evangelical thought can be discerned; the theory emphasized God acting through second causes, while the practical application gave more weight to the idea that God acted more directly.

Simeon, in his book of sermon outlines, *Horae Homilecticae*, noted in his discussion of Matthew 10:30 ("the very hairs of your head are numbered") that it was not the existence of a Supreme Being which was at stake, "but the extent of his agency, and the interest which he takes in the affairs of men". Simeon added: "To imagine a *general* Providence, and to deny or question his *particular* agency in every thing that occurs, is absurd in the extreme. The doctrine of a *particular* Providence is fully confirmed..."[17]

God's omniscience and omnipotence required him to be in control of the whole universe. Scripture showed that all creatures were subject to his control as well as the sun, moon and stars. In relation to society and political economy, when the social questions of poverty and its causes, equality and competition arose, the question was: "Were these to be regarded as beneficent or tragic; as indicators of 'contrivance' by a benevolent and omnipotent Creator, or as the inescapable consequences of the expulsion from Eden?"[18]

The links between Christian theology, Evangelical thought and political economy were achieved through the doctrine of providence. So Adam Smith's "invisible hand" was endowed with divine purpose.

Nineteenth-century Evangelicalism became more open to, and indeed, more specific about the interventionist nature of God. Some of this was linked to the Empire and to the sometimes unfortunate linking of the Empire to the missionary enterprise. Nevertheless, many missionary societies, perhaps pre-eminently the Church Missionary Society, saw themselves as direct instruments in the hands of God for spreading the gospel, and of course, both the Book of Common Prayer and British rule. Evangelical theology underwent something of a transformation in the 1820s,[19] which saw both a greater emphasis upon God's provision of a Protestant constitution for Britain and also a renewed concern for the imminence of the Second Coming. This led to much greater weight being given to the possibility of God's intervention. Key aspects of eschatology (the theology of the end times) supported this more interventionist view of God's action in the world. This included the place of the Jews, the return of Christ, and the place of the miraculous and supernatural gifts. Greater dependence on Christ came to be expressed through prayer (especially at business meetings of, for example, the Bible Society) and through a more passive approach to fundraising for the missionary enterprise. So, for example, the story of Hudson Taylor and the China Inland Mission is one of waiting upon God for his providential financial provision rather than soliciting names for subscription lists, which was the method employed by the more traditional missionary societies. Another example was George Müller of Bristol, the founder of orphanages.

So, then, what place was there in Evangelical thought for the miraculous intervention of God?

From the history we have reviewed so far it will be clear that Evangelicals were cautious about miraculous intervention and yet, following Calvin, wished to maintain a real place for God's continuing providential involvement in his creation and in the lives of his people. This was normally, but not necessarily exclusively achieved through the natural order. Calvin certainly believed that the supernatural gifts and associated offices (apostle, prophet, tongues) belonged only to the apostolic age. Later Evangelicals – including Wesley, Whitefield and other leaders of the movement in the eighteenth and nineteenth centuries – retained this caution but were more explicit about "particular providence". For some, this came to be expressed in a more overt understanding of miracle. There were also some occurrences of and some advocacy of the return of the supernatural gifts. Wesley and Whitefield both described physical signs which accompanied their preaching of the new birth – crying out, weeping, falling down.[20] There were similar occurrences at various outbreaks of revival. There was trembling, ecstatic joy, dancing, even jumping.[21] However, this was not the norm, and the early leaders were cautious in ascribing too much to the phenomena. They explained what was happening in the context of the emotional intensity which was inherent in coming under conviction of sin in the power of the Word – "coming under soul distress" was how Whitefield explained the phenomena.

Similar events took place at Cambuslang near Glasgow, when Whitefield preached to some 30,000 people in the summer of 1742. For some, this was a sign of millennial expectation and the return of Pentecost – but there was no evidence of the Pentecostal gifts. In the 1820s in London, Edward Irving's Church of Scotland congregation became the focus of expectation. Irving, along with many at this time, was advocating a greater dependency upon God and reliance on divine means in mission. After two instances of tongues-speaking in Scotland in the 1830s – which, Bebbington notes, is often given as the first modern occurrence – tongues-speaking broke out in Irving's own London church. These outbreaks did not constitute the norm and neither did they feature in the mainstream of Evangelicalism. Irving fell into Christological heresy and was expelled from the Church of Scotland, founding his own Catholic Apostolic Church. (He became first an angel; his elevation to apostle, we are told, was blocked by a prophet!)

Where, then, does this leave us in considering contemporary Evangelical spiritual practice in respect of providence and the action of God? History offers us three approaches.

First, an adherence to order and a caution towards too ready an ascription to miracle or special interventions. Second, an increasingly greater openness to a more intimate spiritual relationship with God, with more emphasis on divine agency and dependence. This approach retains some caution over miracle and healing. Third, a more explicit embracing of the Pentecostal gifts for today, with an increasing emphasis on signs and power. This expression of spirituality affected some areas of mainstream Evangelicalism, but until recent decades was mainly confined to the emerging denominations of classic Pentecostalism – the Assemblies of God and the Elim Pentecostal churches. In more contemporary spirituality, however, these important elements of devotion and spirituality have entered more fully into the mainstream of Evangelicalism through the Charismatic movement. Indeed, the influence of Charismatic spirituality has extended beyond the traditional boundaries of Evangelicalism even into the Roman Catholic Church.

Now, from providence, let us turn to prayer. Prayer lies at the heart of Christian devotion. However, how prayer works and the practice of prayer reveals some differences among Evangelicals. Can prayer affect the actions of God? Does it make any difference? Philip Yancey refers to a letter he received from a prisoner in Indiana affirming God's providence over the universe, but asking, "does He concern himself at all, to the point of intervention, in our daily trivial lives? Or are His promises of help aimed only at our spiritual self, to help how we respond to events, not to affect events themselves?"[22] If we are able to understand better how Evangelicals have approached prayer, we may be able to improve our contemporary practice of prayer.

Calvin, once again, provides a useful starting point. For Calvin prayer was to do with sustaining the relationship with God. He said, "we dig up by prayer the treasures that were pointed out by the Lord's gospel, and which our faith has gazed upon."[23] This sentence reveals both a central theological strand in Calvin's thought, but also his spiritual depth. There is something of a sense of determinism here: the Lord's promises are set out in his gospel, and prayer brings them to prominence. However, Calvin's reference to unearthing these treasures by prayer and gazing on them through faith invests his understanding of prayer with a degree of devotional depth. He wrote extensively on prayer in his *Institutes*. Prayer, he said, is a response to the command to call upon the Lord's name, so that "our hearts may be fired with a zealous and burning desire ever to seek, love, and serve him, while we become accustomed in every need to flee to him as to a sacred anchor."[24] He adds that prayer keeps us close to God, encourages an attitude of gratitude and confirms his providential care for our lives. Prayer promotes our dependency upon God.

Calvin's exposition formed the basis for later Evangelical thought. The moderate Calvinists of the Church of England stood in this tradition. Prayer was intended to deepen our relationship with God, to lift our hearts in confession of sin, petition and thanksgiving. John Newton commented:

> *I look upon prayer-meetings as the most profitable exercises (excepting the public preaching) in which Christians can engage: they have a direct tendency to kill a worldly, trifling spirit, to draw down a divine blessing upon all our concerns, compose differences, and enkindle (at least to maintain) the flame of divine love amongst brethren.*[25]

Newton, in the light of the Revival, refers to prayer meetings, a rather newer development; as we will see in Chapter 6, it was at these meetings that Newton also introduced hymnody and singing. His theological emphases, however, remained clearly within the Calvinist tradition. However, during the era of the Evangelical Revival prayer did acquire something of a more experiential aspect. The Revival brought into new focus the idea of a personal relationship with God. This brought new emphasis into prayer, not least to intercessory prayer and prayer for conversion. The mission for the conversion of the heathen was not a prominent feature of the Reformers but became an increasingly significant aspect of Evangelicalism, especially into the nineteenth century. This brought a new purpose to intercession.

The Eclectic Society held a discussion on prayer in 1812, quite late on in its existence. The members discussed both the nature and the practice of prayer. One contributor referred to prayer as "the language of the affections towards God" and another added that the "characteristics of true prayer are a sense of need, desire of relief, faith in the divine provisions and promises, patient waiting, longing expectation".[26] We can see here both the continued influence of Calvinism and the more experiential elements of prayer. Patience, waiting and perseverance were also characteristics which would recur in later Evangelical thought.

In practical terms the early Eclectics, who were mainly but not exclusively from the Church of England, were remarkably relaxed. They advocated both vocal and mental prayer and saw walking, kneeling and sitting all as appropriate postures. The habit of prayer was seen as more important than rules or position. As to content, the Eclectics, who were mainly ministers, advocated prayer over the complexities and difficulties of ministry, and prayer for the flock – "the unconverted, the uncertain... backsliders, believers, the mass of unknown."[27] They also advocated an evening a week set aside for intercession. Aware of the problems of complacency, one of the contributors stated that "the spirit of prayer is kept up more by seizing occasions than by dwelling on set subjects."[28] It is clear from these discussions of early Evangelical leaders that there was both a doctrinal clarity over prayer – reflecting the Calvinist heritage – but also a renewed openness and experiential emphasis concerning its practice.

Evangelical prayer life was outwardly focused. Prayer for national life, for government and for the needs of the world all featured prominently. Prayer and Scripture were closely related – reading and meditating on passages of the Bible were prerequisites for effective prayer. Lord Shaftesbury argued that 2 Chronicles should be daily prayed over by every person in public life.[29] John Wesley also reflected this model, but his more Pietist approach at least began to open the door for a more inward focus on prayer. He gave rules for his local societies that they were to pray together and care for each other's spiritual welfare. The prayer was extempore rather than liturgical.[30] Wesley was determined to move prayer away from form and formality, although he did not view genuine prayer as incompatible with liturgy. He was a complex mix of influences. Like all Evangelicals and following Calvin, Wesley was clear that

> *the end of your praying is not to inform God, as though He knew not your wants already; but rather to inform yourselves; to fix the sense of those wants more deeply in your hearts, and the sense of your continual dependence on Him who only is able to supply all your wants. It is not so much to move God, who is always more ready to give than you to ask, as to move yourselves, that you may be willing and ready to receive the good things He has prepared for you.*[31]

What Wesley did – and this was born out in the wider impact of the Revival – was to bring more personal and emotional impact into prayer.

How, then, was prayer perceived to work? In the mainstream Evangelical tradition prayer was understood to work through second causes. This was described by Thomas Chalmers (1780–1847). Chalmers, the Church of Scotland Minister of St John's parish in Glasgow (he left for the Free Church of Scotland in the disruption of 1843), was a renowned preacher and a pioneer of social experiments connected with his opposition to compulsory poor relief in favour of a voluntary system – in other words, philanthropic support for the poor rather than through state intervention. Chalmers clearly aligned himself with the "natural theology"

strand of Evangelical thought. His understanding of the
way in which prayer operated was contained in the second
volume of his *Natural Theology*. His third chapter was entitled
"On the Doctrine of a Special Providence and the Efficacy
of Prayer". Chalmers' basic point was that nature was a
good deal more complex than often understood. Prayer did
not alter the ordered working of the universe, but operated
through second causes. So if there were prayer for wind on
a voyage, and the mariners enjoyed good winds, there was
no miracle, but it was yet God who caused the wind to blow.
At each level of the complex meteorological processes that
gave rise to the wind, the regularities of nature may still be
observed, but ultimately, "there is a hidden intermediate
process which connects the purposes of the divine mind
with the visible phenomena of that universe which He has
created."[32] Thus God answered prayer, but out of sight; yet
he is not banished from the universe.

What difference does prayer make? Can it change God?

The danger of an overemphasis on the classic Calvinist
position of prayer – that is, aligning ourselves with the will
and promises of God, or digging up the treasures already
made explicit by the gospel – is that it can lead to inaction
and reduce prayer to the purely private domain. The
challenge of prayer for the Evangelical is the relationship
between contemplating the will of God and accomplishing
the will of God. Philip Yancey draws attention to two verses
from the Old Testament – Malachi 3:6 ("I the Lord do not
change") and Hosea 11:8 ("My heart is changed within me;

all my compassion is aroused"). How is the paradox resolved by Evangelical Christians?

To help resolve the problem, we first need to understand that humanity was created to have a relationship with God and that prayer is the expression of that relationship. In other words, it is not so much about changing God or changing his mind, but rather about the deepening of a relationship of love. That is why prayer cannot be reduced to petition but involves also confession and thanksgiving. When the Eclectic Society discussed intercession on 8 June 1801, they were clear about the importance and the benefits of intercession. It was a scriptural practice which was to be cultivated. It needed dedicated time: "what can be done at any time, will be done at no time."[33] Intercession has the benefit of enhancing our own mutual affections as we pray for each other and for others – it brings our hearts into a right place, reduces envy and enlarges our vision. What is more, we do not know "what evil is prevented. None know what prayers are answered."[34] John Newton expressed the more classic Calvinist position: "the use of prayer is wholly for one's self, not for God." The reason for that, of course, is that God already possesses full and perfect knowledge of everything and all is predestined in his providence. Newton, however, goes on to say that he himself has experienced answered prayer many times. His vision is characteristically large: "I go round the world sometimes, and intercede for all who know the Lord, at the places on which my thoughts alight."[35]

Perseverance in prayer and the problem of unanswered prayer are related. We are to persevere in prayer because calling on the name of the Lord aligns our hearts ever more closely with God, his ways and his purposes. This is a more fundamental rationale for prayer than seeking answers to particular needs. Prayer is informed by need, but the inscrutable ways of God are not for us to know. The manner of answered prayer is a matter for God alone. In fact it is God's unchanging character which gives us confidence that he will hear prayer and answer. So the purpose of intercession is to bring people and desires before him as we are commanded to do, not to twist his arm, but to plead, that our will may reflect that of his divine majesty.

Prayer and power

However, it is also easy to see how such an approach might be deemed inadequate. In the next chapter we will explore the development of the holiness movement in the nineteenth century and the beginnings of Pentecostalism. With these developments, and a new approach to sanctification and the Christian life, prayer did become more inwardly focused and, to some degree, more world-denying. The shift also was towards prayer understood in terms of "Spirit-filled power".

The Pentecostal movement and, more recently, the neo-Pentecostal Charismatic movement, have brought more emphasis on the place of prayer in spiritual warfare. This builds upon the ideas from Ephesians that the Christian is involved in a battle against evil forces. Although Satan has long been a focus of Evangelical prayer, the idea of "spiritual warfare" is relatively recent. It gives weight to the power motif in prayer but it carries considerable danger. An over-realized view of demons, evil spirits and territorial spirits brings much danger of dualism – that is, of denying God's sovereignty over the world and the universe by posing his sovereignty to be in some form of equal conflict with evil. This approach to prayer is the same one that gives emphasis to healing, miracle and the Pentecostal gifts.

The final area of the Christian life to reflect upon more explicitly is the question of guidance. How does God guide? In a sense, we can see from the discussion of providence, prayer and call, that God guides the individual believer through a combination of these factors. Prayer brings the believer closer to God and aligns their will with his; God answers prayer or works out his purposes through providential acts. In practical terms, we saw this very well illustrated in the lives of some of those whose call and vocation we described in Chapter 3.

Contemporary Evangelical practice

Contemporary practice has much to learn from the variety of traditions which make up the mosaic of Evangelicalism. Few Evangelicals today have a particularly deep understanding of prayer. The church would benefit from teaching on the subject of prayer and providence, how God acts and how we are called to devote ourselves to him. For some, this lack of teaching has left prayer as a perfunctory exercise ("Lord, thank you for this food, bless those that have none," before the sumptuous meal), or a dry recitation, or a simple listing of desires. Elsewhere within Evangelicalism the idea of Spirit-filled power prayer has been embraced with much enthusiasm and excitement, and certainly has brought a powerful reminder of confidence and expectancy. However, this emphasis has much to explain in terms of disappointment and can embrace a theology that sees the miraculous as normative rather than exceptional.

The more Charismatic strand of Evangelicalism may

advocate a wider range of prayer practices. This may include a variety of postures (stand, kneel, lie down), accompanying practices such as fasting, varieties of method (vocal, quiet) and some weight given to power, expressed perhaps in prayer for healing. The mainstream Evangelical tradition can learn from its history why some of these emphases are adopted by some (but not all), and also recognize the significant and powerful contribution that this strand of the tradition makes. Evangelical leaders will express caution about the danger of dualism in some of the more excessive expressions of spiritual warfare, and of a sometimes over-realized eschatology in respect of miracle.

The more Reformed elements of the Evangelical tradition call us to focus upon God, his majesty, his sovereignty, his will and his promises. The whole concept of aligning ourselves with God and his promises and his will is powerful. Confession, petition and thanksgiving, and indeed a very wide view of God's rule over the world, feature strongly in this tradition.

Setting aside the fact that different parts of the Evangelical tradition will embrace somewhat different emphases, Evangelicals will want together to give weight to personal prayer, to prayer for the conversion of the unbeliever, to intercession, struggle, wrestling and perseverance in prayer. This prayer will flow into the Christian life, reflected in a life of dependency, seeking God's will and guidance, recognizing his providential hand, but also giving ourselves wholly over to him and offering up to him our praise and thanksgiving.

We began with the problem of prayer for the parking space or the middle-class ailment and how our expectation of an answer to these prayers matches up to evil in the world. Why would God heal backache in Reigate, but not prevent the Holocaust? At the close of this chapter we can conclude that both those prayers may be appropriate. God, in his divine providence, can indeed answer such prayer, though we may not see that answer or understand how he might do so. That is not ours to ask. To pray for those needs as part of a whole life of prayer and a deepening relationship with God, and then trusting in him for the answer, is indeed an appropriate spiritual practice. So is to pray against evil and to recognize that human sin has a significant role in the practice of evil in the world. We must avoid the dualism of seeing evil as some sort of independent force. We also need to remind ourselves of the power of sin and the call to struggle against sin and evil, and above all, to intercede, that the Lord may deliver us, and turn to himself those whom he is calling.

Notes

1. John Calvin, *Institutes of the Christian Religion*, 1559, Library of Christian Classics, ed. J. T. McNeil, 2 volumes, Philadelphia: Westminster Press, 1960, I.5.11.
2. Roger Anstey, *The Atlantic Slave Trade and British Abolition*, London: Macmillan, 1975, p. 174.
3. Calvin, *Institutes*, I.5.2.
4. Calvin, *Institutes*, I.16.1.
5. Calvin, *Institutes*, I.16.2.
6. Calvin, *Institutes*, I.16.4.
7. R. Porter and M. Teich, *The Enlightenment in National Context*, Cambridge: CUP, 1981, p. 16.
8. David Bebbington, *Evangelicalism in Modern Britain*, London: Unwin Hyman, 1989, pp. 50–74.
9. Anstey, *Atlantic Slave Trade*, p. 160.
10. J. H. Pratt, *The Thought of the Evangelical Leaders*, 1856, Edinburgh: Banner of Truth Trust, 1978, p. 485.
11. Pratt, *Thought of the Evangelical Leaders*, p. 495.
12. Pratt, *Thought of the Evangelical Leaders*, p. 495.

13. William Wilberforce, *A Practical View*, 1797, chapter VI, p. 422.

14. Pratt, *Thought of the Evangelical Leaders*, p. 468.

15. Pratt, *Thought of the Evangelical Leaders*, p. 486.

16. Pratt, *Thought of the Evangelical Leaders*, p. 501.

17. Charles Simeon, *Horae Homilecticae* (21 vols, 1832–33), vol. 11, p. 325.

18. A. M. C. Waterman, "The Ideological Alliance of Political Economy and Christian Theology, 1798–1833", *Journal of Ecclesiastical History*, vol. 34, no. 2, April 1983, p. 231.

19. Richard Turnbull, *Shaftesbury: The Great Reformer*, Oxford: Lion, pp. 32–34.

20. Mark Noll, *The Rise of Evangelicalism*, Leicester: Apollos, 2004, p. 91.

21. D. Bruce Hindmarsh, *The Evangelical Conversion Narrative*, Oxford: OUP, 2005, pp. 133–35.

22. Philip Yancey, *Prayer*, London: Hodder & Stoughton, 2006, p. 64.

23. Calvin, *Institutes*, III.20.2.

24. Calvin, *Institutes*, III.20.3.

25. John Newton, quoted in G. Mursell, *English Spirituality, From Earliest Times to 1700*, London: SPCK, 2008, p. 28.

26. Pratt, *Thought of the Evangelical Leaders*, p. 514.

27. Pratt, *Thought of the Evangelical Leaders*, p. 513.

28. Pratt, *Thought of the Evangelical Leaders*, p. 514.

29. Turnbull, *Shaftesbury*, p. 213.

30. Mursell, *English Spirituality*, pp. 89–90.

31. Quoted in Mursell, *English Spirituality*, p. 96.

32. Thomas Chalmers, *Natural Theology*, in *Works*, 25 volumes, Glasgow: W. Collins & Son, 1836–1842, vol. 2, p. 118.

33. Pratt, *Thought of the Evangelical Leaders*, p. 229.

34. Pratt, *Thought of the Evangelical Leaders*, p. 229.

35. Pratt, *Thought of the Evangelical Leaders*, p. 230.

5

Holiness and Sanctification

....

The idea of God's providential hand over the Christian life, sustained by a life of prayer and dependency upon God, has been one of the main strands of the Evangelical spiritual life. The praise and thanks to God which is the natural response of the heart is expressed in worship and praise, which we will look at in more detail in Chapter 6.

These basic elements of the Evangelical spiritual life led to further developments in the quest for living of a holy life. Wesley and some (but not all) of the early Evangelicals were influenced by "orthodox high churchmanship" represented by the writings of Jeremy Taylor (*The Rule and Exercises of Holy Living*) and William Law (*A Serious Call to a Devout and Holy Life*). This pursuit was then reinterpreted within Evangelicalism. What was the place of holiness within the life of the convert? The answer revealed differences in the approach to sanctification – that is, the doctrine of the transformation of the Christian life.

The classic Reformed tradition, in both its high Calvinist and more moderate forms (the latter characterized and shaped the Revival within the Church of England), viewed sanctification, firstly, as separate from justification and, secondly, as a gradual process of constant struggle against indwelling sin. Wesley changed the terms of the debate, even if his advocacy of the possibility of Christian perfectionism did not gain traction within mainstream Evangelicalism in the eighteenth century. He laid the groundwork for later developments with the growth of the holiness movement in the nineteenth century, which profoundly influenced the mainstream Evangelical spiritual tradition as well as preparing the way for later Pentecostal expressions of holiness.

The essential contrast revolved around whether sanctification was gradual or sudden. Wesley prevaricated, but for the holiness movement the emphasis was placed upon a sudden crisis of faith leading to the second blessing and the higher Christian life.

Classic sanctification

The close links – albeit noting some nuances and developments – between the Reformed heritage of Calvinism and the mainstream Evangelical spiritual tradition have been one of our themes. Although the Revival brought new emphases, it did so primarily in continuity with the antecedent Reformed tradition. Sanctification, however, emerged as a contested area.

Bebbington notes the traditional Evangelical view as espoused by Hannah More, which he refers to as "steady plodding".[1] According to this view, the Christian life for the Evangelical was one lived in constant friction with sin – a struggle, a battle, a conflict. For John Newton this amounted to nothing less than spiritual warfare; the contest would be hard fought and costly, and would require great courage, but ultimately the Christian would be victorious – ultimately, but not immediately. Grace was needed daily for the conflict with sin and there would be disappointment and failure along the way, but trust in Christ would ultimately deliver. Prayer and the development of Christian character, living not by law but certainly within scriptural ethical norms, provide the framework of the Christian quest for holiness. So, the Christian life required quite a lot of the "steady plodding" that Bebbington refers to, and it is easy to see how this classic Puritan approach could be seen as more burden than release in the light of the new birth.

The Puritan classic in which this spiritual tradition is most strongly represented is John Bunyan's *The Pilgrim's Progress*. Perhaps the title speaks for itself. The narrative is the story of the pilgrim, Christian, and his journey through life to heaven (represented by the Celestial City). The narrative is primarily *after* the burden of sin has been lifted at Calvary. The story involves all the ups and downs, temptations, struggles, battles and encouragements of the Christian life. Christian faces onslaught from every side (the character is probably a personification of Bunyan himself). Sin and temptation are represented by marvellously named characters such as Giant Despair, Mr Malice, Mr Liar and Mr Hate-light, and life's dark alleyways by place-names such as the Valley of the Shadow of Death, the Hill of Difficulty and Vanity Fair. Christian, however, is helped on his journey to the Celestial City by Faithful and Hopeful and the regular appearance of Evangelist. The sole objective of life is the journey to the eternal city. The sustenance for the journey comes from reliance on Scripture. The story brings out the key themes of Puritan spirituality – the daily struggle against sin and temptation, and the centrality of Scripture in guiding and shaping the Christian life.

The advent of the Revival and the development of new movements of holiness meant that alternative positions vied for the attention of the Christian public in the nineteenth century. However, the classic position still had its exponents. J. C. Ryle, the Bishop of Liverpool from 1880, wrote (in 1879) his masterpiece *Holiness* as an exposition of the continuing relevance of the classic teaching. His stated aim was to bring about "a thorough revival about *Scriptural holiness*".[2] Ryle's exposition of his subject began with sin. Like Edwards a century before, Ryle's understanding of the traditional doctrine began with humanity's depravity and the all-pervasive nature of indwelling sin. He went on to describe practical holiness as the habit of being of one mind with God in the endeavour to shun sin, keep the law of the Lord and strive to be like Christ. Other characteristics followed: meekness, self-denial, purity, humility and so on. Subsequent chapters of Ryle's classic were called "The Fight" and "The Cost". The entire framework was that of the classic Calvinist struggle against sin and to be like Christ.

In more recent times the work of J. I. Packer has stood in this Reformed tradition. *Knowing God* was first published in 1973. He described the book as a treatise on God. He was concerned with God's majesty, kingship, salvation and holiness. Godliness, Packer argued, "means responding to God's revelation in trust and obedience, faith and worship, prayer and praise, submission and service. Life must be seen and lived in the light of God's Word. This, and nothing else, is true religion."[3] In 1992 he published *A Passion for Holiness*, in which he surveyed holiness and reflected on the idea of an empowered spiritual life. He argued that the Christian life is a test of endurance, a long-distance race involving struggle and suffering.

Wesleyan perfectionism

John and Charles Wesley both reacted strongly against Calvinist teaching. This was true not only in respect of redemption – salvation was available for all who turned to Christ, not just the elect – but also in terms of living the Christian life. John Wesley believed that there was a second stage of sanctification available, subsequent to conversion, in which the believer could achieve a total victory over sin, a total death to sin, and which would result in the overflowing of prayer and thanksgiving. This was the essence of "Christian perfection", a gift of God in faith, a status which Wesley himself never claimed, but one in which the Christian was freed not only from sinful acts, but also from sinful thought and temptation. As Bebbington points out, it was only possible for some Wesleyans to claim perfection through a redefinition of sin to a voluntary transgression of a known law; or to put it another way, the unconscious and ignorant error was not sin.[4] Otherwise, it was too difficult. Wesley referred to this state of Christian holiness as "perfect love". This idea certainly challenged concepts of original sin. The matter was a complex one, made more so by the language (did "perfection" mean perfection?). The teaching was controversial in Wesley's own time, and into the middle of the nineteenth century the doctrine remained largely within Methodism, and even there came to be adapted and perhaps even dissipated.

For Wesley, the emphasis was not so much on perfection as on giving – devotion to God of the heart, the body and the soul. In fact, total self-giving. Gordon Mursell has summed up Wesley's quest: "Perfection, then, is total self-giving. The difficulty is that the term can also imply a static sense of sinlessness, which is what upset many contemporaries."[5]

Wesley was open to the charge of advocating the possibility of the sinless life, though he insisted this was not the case and he generally resisted the view that perfection was possible instantaneously. For him, crisis and process were intertwined. Wesley was quite careful in his own writings, but left the door open. "Perfection" was a slippery word. The emphasis was on constant communion with God, becoming Christ-like, regaining the whole image of God, having the mind of Christ, or as Wesley put it, "walking as Christ walked".[6] It was the work of the Spirit that purified and sanctified the soul. Christians were then set free to live as his children. To love God, to be transformed into his likeness and to do his will lay at the heart of Wesley's idea of Christian perfection.

This was not a sterile doctrine, but it was misunderstood and, almost certainly, was also rather misplaced. Wesley claimed to have known hundreds who had the experience of Christian perfection. Certainly, if perfection was expressed in terms of love for God and the desire to bear fruit towards humanity, few would have disagreed. Wesley, however, added the phrase "attended with power over all sin" to his description of perfection.[7] At this point not all went along with him. To Wesley, perfection was a biblical word and the doctrine as he expounded it was scriptural. He argued in some places that sanctification was possible in an instant as an act of faith, and elsewhere he continued to argue that there remained a process and a gradual work. Despite this complexity, Wesley positioned himself self-consciously against the Calvinist (and the mainstream Evangelical) position of constant struggle and gradual sanctification. He argued that he could not believe that God had sent us into the world to be miserable! The

Methodist classes and bands also had select groups for those furthest advanced on the road to Christian perfection. In this Wesley was something of a precursor to later developments of Christians seeking the higher life or the second blessing, to which we now turn. He left a door certainly ajar, if not wide open, that classic Evangelical spirituality had always regarded as firmly closed.

Keswick holiness

In periods when the fires of revival burn low, or at least not at the same intensity as when the Spirit of God moves across the land, there is often an intense desire to increase the emphasis on personal holiness. Before revival can return, the thinking goes, God demands purity. By the middle of the nineteenth century, Evangelicalism was well established, but was clearly into the second generation. Thus some of the early pioneering spirit had been lost, at least in the eyes of some enthusiasts. This was the era of campaigns, societies and perhaps even the institutionalization of the movement. From around 1836, Phoebe Palmer organized meetings in her New York home for the promotion of holiness. She was the wife of a Methodist doctor and became interested in Wesleyan teaching on Christian perfection. Her sister was also involved in the promotion of "entire sanctification", as the teaching was known. Her "altar theology", seeing everything in life laid upon the altar which is Christ, characterized her holiness teaching. This was an act of the will, linking the teaching into the wider movement of Romanticism – an intellectual trend that reacted against rationalism and gave weight to the emotions and experience. Palmer emphasized faith, even more than the traditional Wesleyan stress on experience. She deeply influenced William and Catherine Booth, so preparing the way for the later emphasis on holiness within the Salvation Army.

The new teaching on holiness and sanctification strongly affected Evangelicalism, particularly from about 1870 onwards. Various forms of language were used to describe both the process and the impact. The objective was to achieve some form of "second blessing" of the Spirit which would lead to "entire sanctification" or the "higher life". Although this teaching was related to Wesley's teaching on perfection and laid the groundwork for later Pentecostalism, the emphasis was distinct from both. The new teaching focused on "rest", "surrender" and "victory" rather than the traditional motifs of struggle, conflict and effort. The "higher life" was a gift of faith from God rather than a consequence of struggle. Many of these emphases found their place within the mainstream of the Evangelical tradition, not least expressed in its hymnody, but also in the development of teaching conferences for scriptural holiness, the most prominent of which, from 1875, was Keswick. As well as the Salvation Army, the movement also deeply affected evangelists such as D. L. Moody.

Among the forerunners of Keswick holiness was the Mildmay Movement. William Pennefather, while incumbent of Christ Church, Barnet, and later St Jude's, Mildmay Park, convened conferences for Christian workers from 1856. By 1869 attendance was approaching 1,000. Many of the themes of holiness were taught at Mildmay. Although there was considerable Anglican influence (which helped ensure that holiness teaching was not detached from Calvinism), the Mildmay Conference was interdenominational and attracted both Brethren and Quaker support. Pennefather stressed the work of the Spirit, the need for purity, perhaps even separation from the world, but held back from a particular line on sanctification. The piety was intense but many Mildmay speakers, both before and after the development of holiness teaching, resisted the message of entire sanctification. These conferences instituted a new phenomenon into Evangelical piety – conferences and conventions.

The key initiators of the holiness movement in Britain were an American couple, Robert and Hannah Pearsall Smith. They addressed holiness conferences in 1874–75 in Oxford and Brighton. They built upon the idea of faith – dependency upon God was to be the characteristic of the ordinary believer's Christian life, just as much as in the interdenominational faith missions. Indeed, Hudson Taylor of the China Inland Mission embraced the principles of holiness. There was also much affinity with the increasingly dominant theme of Christ's premillennial advent. All of this was, of course, also an expression of the Romanticism of the age. As Bebbington comments, "the sensibility of the age… lay behind the new spiritual language."[8]

The setting of Keswick (described by Bebbington as "a novel and potent style of spirituality")[9] was, of course, essential and indeed highly conducive to Victorian Romanticism. Set amid the lakes and the mountains, the convention participants were surrounded by clouds, sun, rain and the poetry of William Wordsworth. Nature was consecrated. Idealism, escapism and holiness were all rolled into one. The Romantic movement found its religious outlet in the holiness movement. The emphasis on the individual, upon power, the higher life, being lifted, offering, emotion, the affections, the will and the heart – all these themes were expressed. The holiness movement offered rest from the daily struggle against sin. Romanticism generally, and holiness teaching in particular, represented something of an escape from reality for the Evangelical, fleeing from the twin juggernauts of rationalism and ritualism, but also from the constant struggle of the Christian life against sin. In the light of such conflicts, the quest for a purer and higher spirituality was very appealing. Bebbington quotes one clerical attendee at a holiness conference as seeking "the secret of the spiritual power which some of my brethren possess".[10] Power became something of a theme – it was picked up later by both classic Pentecostalism and the neo-Pentecostalist Charismatic movement. These elements formed part of an increasingly prominent revivalist network which, certainly at the margins, embraced Arminianism and rejected traditional Calvinism. We will look at that in more detail in Chapter 7.

Opponents of the holiness movement regarded it as shallow, emotional, lacking doctrinal weight, sentimental and pietistic. Indeed, to cease to struggle against sin opened the door to moral laxity – to antinomianism. This point was emphasized by Robert Pearsall Smith's indiscretions with a young woman that saw him leave Britain for America once again – the victory over sin was clearly not quite complete in his case. Indeed, as with many "lifestyle" movements, it was made clear that doctrine was not an area of concern. Hannah Pearsall Smith was well known as a universalist.[11] The movement suffered much from the danger of relativism (the irony of this in a movement designed to enhance purity is noted by Bebbington)[12] – sin, as with Wesley, became reduced to known transgressions, perhaps even publicly known errors. If knowledge of sin remained private, there was even a danger of moral relativism – or at least self-justification for moral failure. The same tone made some more sympathetic to mystical teaching, including Roman Catholicism – anathema, of course, to most Evangelicals. Ryle questioned whether the contemporary holiness movement placed sufficient weight on practical discipline in daily life. He doubted the role of faith alone in sanctification (as opposed to justification). He resisted the idea of perfection and queried the exegesis of Romans 7, arguing that the chapter refers to the struggles of the Christian rather than humanity in its unregenerate state. He doubted some of the contemporary spiritual language and resisted the separation of conversion and consecration (or the higher life). Finally, he rejected the language of "yielding" in favour of fight and struggle against sin. He summarized his position thus (while still in his introduction!):

> *But the plain truth is, that men will persist in confounding two things that differ – that is, justification and sanctification. In justification the word to be addressed to man is believe – only believe; in sanctification the word must be "watch, pray, and fight." What God has divided let us not mingle and confuse.*[13]

Indeed, the onslaught against entire sanctification was such that the concept received less and less attention in Keswick teaching. The mainstream wished to maintain much of traditional moderate Calvinism. Others wished to move beyond that and found their outlet in Pentecostalism. The Keswick Convention came to adopt a position of the conjuncture of crisis and process – that is, a combination of the two. Calvinists (including Bishop Ryle) remained suspicious, but it protected the movement from the more marginal and extreme expressions of holiness. Keswick teaching insisted that perfection was not possible and that sin could not be entirely removed from the Christian life this side of the Second Advent. Ryle endorsed Moody but rejected the teaching of Pearsall Smith; a discerning judgment. He described the difference between them as that between sunshine and fog.[14]

The beginnings of Pentecostalism

The roots of Pentecostalism are varied and more complex than sometimes suggested.[15] The multiplicity of influences included Wesleyan perfectionism, the holiness movement, historic examples of *glossolalia* (that is, speaking in tongues) and the Welsh Revival of 1904–5. However, modern scholars usually point in the first instance to Charles Fox Parham in Kansas and, subsequently, Houston, who linked the baptism of the Spirit with the gift of tongues. Parham and one of his pupils, Agnes Ozman, received the gift in 1901. This then prepared the way for the phenomenon to reach Los Angeles.

The nineteenth century closed with the holiness emphasis preparing the way for the renewal of tongues in the Pentecostal outpouring at Azusa Street in Los Angeles in 1906, followed by the experience of Alexander Boddy in Sunderland. The initial contest for a view of the "second blessing" that allowed for tongues took place at Keswick. Some participants were disappointed that Keswick did not embrace the phenomenon. In fact, speaking in tongues as a sign of the second blessing of the Spirit was rejected by Keswick and the wider holiness movement. If the "higher life" and "complete sanctification" of Keswick holiness set the scene, it was certainly insufficient for some. The Pentecostal outpouring arrived in Britain in Sunderland, in the north-east of England, through a visit of T. B. Barratt to Boddy's church, All Saints, Monkwearmouth in 1907. Barratt had been in touch with Azusa Street and received the gift of tongues while in New York. Boddy was influenced by the Welsh Revival – which strongly reflected holiness teaching, though there is no reliable evidence for tongues-speaking.[16] He had also been an active participant in Keswick but was frustrated by the caution over *glossolalia*. One reason for the rejection of tongues-speaking was that the phenomenon was seen by some not simply as an occasional outpouring of the Spirit or an accompaniment to revival, but as the one sure sign of Spirit-baptism. The differences are illustrated by James Robinson who notes that where "Keswick majored on 'victory,' and 'resting in the Lord,' Pentecostals took the American Higher Life position that stressed 'power for service.'"[17]

The Christian life – both higher and lower

The manner of how the Christian life is lived, in particular the nature and process of sanctification, became a distinctive feature of Evangelical piety in the second half of the nineteenth century. A great strength of the holiness movement was that it demonstrated over time that some of the key spiritual emphases it brought did not necessarily lead to a rejection of classic Calvinism. So, although in the more conservative parts of the Evangelical tradition there will be a vigorous reassertion of the classic approach to sanctification and holiness, the mainstream has embraced some aspects of the holiness movement. This is perhaps the "later Keswick" rather than the earlier, adopting the themes of sacrifice and dependency, welcoming the holiness hymnody but resisting perfectionism and crisis sanctification. Those latter emphases have remained more prominent within the Pentecostal and Charismatic spiritual traditions.

It is perhaps in the area of spiritual disciplines that the differences emerge in practice. Ironically, there are some contradictions. Practices such as fasting, the adoption of particular bodily postures, and certain mystical practices (perhaps even tongue-speaking in prayer) are more likely to be observed in the Pietist/Revivalist axis that emphasizes the holiness tradition. This may give the impression of the very human means which the tradition has sought to resist. Perhaps here, in contemporary practice, is also where there remains stress on the second blessing or being filled with the Spirit, though it should be noted that neither tongues (classic Pentecostalism) nor prophecy and pictures (neo-Pentecostalism) were ever envisaged by the Keswick holiness tradition.

The classic end of the spectrum will stress ethics, the disciplines of Bible study and prayer, distrust of experience, and the reading of the Reformed spiritual classics.

Most of Evangelicalism can unite in hymnody, prayer, dependence in faith, humility and service. The mainstream tradition remains firmly rooted in its moderate Calvinism; it expresses its spirituality through both the quest for the higher life and the practice of the humble lower spiritual life of service and discipleship.

Notes

....

1. David Bebbington, *Evangelicalism in Modern Britain*, London: Unwin Hyman, 1989, p. 169.
2. J. C. Ryle, *Holiness*, London: James Clarke & Co., 1956, p. vii.
3. J. I. Packer, *Knowing God*, Downers Grove, Illinois: IVP, 20th anniversary edition, 1993, p. 20.
4. Bebbington, *Evangelicalism*, p. 153.
5. G. Mursell, *English Spirituality, From Earliest Times to 1700*, London: SPCK, 2008, p. 93.
6. Mursell, *English Spirituality*, p. 94.
7. James Gordon, *Evangelical Spirituality*, London: SPCK, 1991, p. 29.
8. Bebbington, *Evangelicalism*, p. 152.
9. David Bebbington, *The Dominance of Evangelicalism*, Leicester: IVP, 2005, p. 195.
10. Bebbington, *Evangelicalism*, p. 152.
11. Bebbington, *Evangelicalism*, p. 171.
12. Bebbington, *Evangelicalism*, p. 168.
13. Ryle, *Holiness*, p. xvii.
14. Bebbington, *Evangelicalism*, p. 171.
15. Mursell, *English Spirituality*, p. 405.
16. K. Warrington (ed.), *Pentecostal Perspectives*, Carlisle: Paternoster Press, 1998, p. 2.
17. James Robinson, *Pentecostal Origins*, Milton Keynes: Paternoster, 2005, p. 11.

6

Worship and Hymnody

Greatly disgusted at the manner of singing.
1. Twelve or fourteen persons kept it to themselves,
and quite shut out the congregation; 2. These
repeated the same words, contrary to all sense and
reason, six or eight times over; 3. According to the
shocking custom of modern music, different persons
sang different words at one and the same moment;
an intolerable insult on common sense, and utterly
incompatible with any devotion. [1]

....

Perhaps this is a minister fed up with the choir, or complaining of the excessive repetition of a music group? In fact, these are the words of John Wesley in 1768! The complaint illustrates the complexity of the history of the musical tradition as it has developed within Evangelical spirituality. Wesley was complaining about the musicians, who were using contemporary tunes to accompany psalms, while the congregation listened. To correct such deficiencies (in their view), both John and Charles Wesley wrote vast quantities of hymns for congregational participation. Estimates for the output from Charles alone range from 4,000 to 9,000, with some 3,000 still extant. [2]

Understanding something of the nature and development of hymnody within worship and how it developed within the Evangelical tradition helps us appreciate the changing and complex role of the hymn or sacred song in Evangelical spirituality. By considering the origin, content and use of hymns we are able to assess both their significance and something of the nature of the tensions that can arise within this aspect of Evangelical devotion.

Hymns did not originate with the Evangelical Revival but through it they were invested with a renewed significance. Hymns were adopted by "dissenting" congregations before those of the Established Church. They were subsequently embraced by Church of England Evangelicals, but not generally in church services until the nineteenth century. Hymns were a key means of conveying doctrine, and the beliefs asserted depended not only on the author but also on the ecclesiastical tradition. In the nineteenth century hymns became something of a battleground between competing theological convictions, including Tractarian[3] sympathizers who rose to some significance within the Church of England. The various spiritual strands of Evangelicalism reflected some changing emphases within hymnody and this prepared the way for more modern developments. These recent shifts include instrumental and temperamental variety, but also a change in the way in which we view the purpose of hymns and songs. The classic position was that church members sang hymns to each other in praise of God, but more Charismatic spirituality would give weight to sacred song as being a gateway to intimacy with God. Simply recognizing the difference helps to explain variety of practice. By the latter part of the nineteenth century the holiness movement and Victorian Romanticism combined with classic Evangelicalism to personalize hymnody once again (that is, to give weight to the personal devotional aspects of singing – "Take my life and let it be…") and prepare the way for more contemporary expressions within twentieth-century neo-Pentecostalism.

There are two conflicting tensions in the development of music in church worship in the early part of the eighteenth century. The musical accompaniment was provided by a rather ad hoc group of village musicians. They gathered in the gallery at the west end of the parish church for Sunday worship. Using a variety of instruments, they played simple folk tunes and led the singing. In essence it was the village band. Slowly, but surely, they were ousted by the organ, or the harmonium. The choir now appeared in the chancel rather than the gallery, more directly under the control of the clergy. This development was viewed negatively by a number of commentators; at worst, it was seen as a means of social control over the working class. Thus far it sounds rather like a modern contemporary music group, suppressed in the high nineteenth century and recovered in the late twentieth.

However, to describe the other aspects of the picture reveals the complexity. Singing in most churches – and all churches which were part of the Church of England – in the seventeenth and eighteenth centuries actually consisted only of psalms. The singing was led by a parish clerk (or precentor) who would sing a line which was repeated by the assembled musicians in the gallery (known as "lining-out"). The congregation listened passively. The gallery musicians, often arriving late, rarely approached their task spiritually; they were indeed the village singers, sometimes the worse for drink, usually hiding behind the gallery curtain except for their own set part, reading, playing cards and engaging in gossip during the sermon. So this part of the description sounds like a modern minister's "worst-case scenario" description of conflict between the minister and the traditional choir.

Thomas Hardy, within the text of *Under the Greenwood Tree*, describes the rural parish of Mellstock around 1840. He relates the last days of the "west gallery" music tradition, which continued in rural parishes into the mid nineteenth century. His comments in the preface to the 1896 edition revealed his own concerns:

> *One is inclined to regret the displacement of these ecclesiastical bandsmen by an isolated organist (often at first a barrel-organist) or harmonium player; and despite certain advantages in point of control and accomplishment... its direct result being to curtain and extinguish the interests of parishioners in church doings.*[4]

In seeking to understand how Evangelicals have approached hymnody, we need to remember that the appeal of the old village band and singers as described by Hardy was limited because they displayed many of the characteristics which today have sometimes been associated with what replaced the west gallery tradition – robed choirs.

Hymns – as we know them today – were not permitted within the worship of the Church of England until after 1819 and were slow to catch on, even though they were embraced by the church's Evangelical wing. The position outside of the Church of England was not dissimilar. Most congregations used psalms, like their more established colleagues. The principal historical reason for this was that the Reformation in England – both within the Established Church and outside of it – owed more to Geneva than Wittenburg. In other words,

English church worship reflected John Calvin's commitment to only singing sacred Scripture more than Martin Luther's passion for congregational singing. However, progress towards a more general use of hymnody did advance more quickly outside the Church of England than within it, with a noticeable area of overlap brought about by the Revival.

The most significant example of an exception to the general trend is of considerable importance. Isaac Watts (1674–1748) was the pioneer of Evangelical hymnody. Watts was a dissenter, the Minister of Mark Lane independent chapel in London from 1702 until his death, and the author of some 700 hymns.[5] He introduced some new tunes for traditional psalm singing, but he went further by writing new spiritual poetry for use for congregational singing. His hymns are probably the finest examples in the period prior to the Revival and the Wesleyan era. We see in Watts' compositions a foretaste of some of the themes and purposes of hymnody within Evangelical spirituality. Singing in dissenting chapels other than the psalms had been permitted from 1689 – due to the freedom allowed for under the Toleration Act – but the practice was slow to catch on. Perhaps Watts' most famous hymn was "Crucifixion to the World by the Cross of Christ, Gal. vi.14", published in his *Hymns and Spiritual Songs* (1707). We know the hymn today as "When I survey the wondrous cross". Here it is in its original form:

> *When I survey the wondrous cross,*
> *Where the young Prince of Glory dy'd,*
> *My richest gain I count but loss,*
> *And pour contempt on all my pride.*
> *Forbid it, Lord, that I should boast,*
> *Save in the death of Christ my God;*

> *All the vain things that charm me most,*
> *I sacrifice them to his blood.*[6]

We see here the beginnings of the personalization of hymns – the personal pronoun became increasingly prominent, and the debate has continued to the present day. We see also the characteristics of the cross, the atonement and the conveying of doctrine through hymns. Some of these themes remained constant as time went on; others changed, as we will see. Watts is the prime exemplar of an early Evangelical hymn-writer. "Joy to the World", "Jesus shall reign where'er the sun" and "O God, our help in ages past" were also among his offerings. Watts had a broad vision of God. As well as the cross, nature featured strongly in his hymns (e.g. "And heaven and nature sing" from "Joy to the World"), as does the whole concept of assurance:

> *O God, our help in ages past,*
> *Our hope for years to come,*
> *Our shelter from the stormy blast,*
> *And our eternal home.*

Today we often remember a hymn or song by its tune. This was not the case prior to the mid nineteenth century. In that period specific tunes were not attached to particular hymns, and the hymn-writer concentrated on the poetry of the words and their spiritual significance. The early hymns and psalms were sung to a variety of melodies. Indeed, it was a characteristic of the west gallery tradition (and, to some, an example of its disorder) that the psalms and, in some places, the hymns were sung to a variety of popular tunes.

Within the Evangelical part of the Church of England

there was a rather mixed reception for the new hymns. As hymns began to be a feature of Methodist bands (i.e. local societies), their attractive and powerful impact could not be foresworn by Anglican Evangelicals. Some of those most closely associated with Methodism began to introduce hymn-singing – illegally at first. However, the Established Church Evangelicals tended to remain committed to the psalm-singing tradition. This reflected, somewhat at least, their Calvinistic theology, compared to the Wesleyan Arminianism. However, John Newton, who, with the poet William Cowper, produced the *Olney Hymnbook* (1779), introduced congregational hymn-singing at Olney in three mid-week prayer meetings. However, he did not do so for Sunday worship. The *Olney Hymnbook* was remarkable. The theology of Newton and the poetry of Cowper made a powerful combination. Newton was Cowper's pastor and the poet had a history of depression and struggle with his faith. This contributed to the feel of the hymnbook. Cowper contributed around one fifth of the nearly 350 hymns in the original edition; the rest were from Newton's pen. The hymns covered Christian truth and personal experience, including that of Cowper himself and his struggles. They had a rather different theological feel from those of Charles Wesley.

The singing of spiritual songs or hymns advanced most speedily among Methodist groups and dissenting congregations. The single most prolific author of hymns in the Revival was Charles Wesley. These hymns became the key means by which doctrine and teaching was conveyed to the various constituencies arising out of the Revival. Hymns carried a number of distinctive features and were used as polemical means for the advocacy or defence of particular doctrines. This was true for pioneers such as Isaac Watts and

Charles Wesley, and it was also the case into the nineteenth century and beyond.

Charles Wesley's hymns continue to occupy a significant place in the piety of Evangelicals, as part of the wider picture of spiritual hymnody. Some of Wesley's grand, expansive hymns (for example, "O for a thousand tongues to sing") were written specifically for the open-air rallies and preaching undertaken by the Wesley brothers. The Wesleys published collections of hymns, and Cowper and Newton issued the *Olney Hymnbook*, but the hymnbook as we know it today was largely a Victorian invention. Changes to the lyrics were not unusual; hymnbooks were big business.

Charles Wesley's hymns could fall into romantic and esoteric fantasy – his brother John described some of them as "namby-pambical".[7] There were inevitably some examples of poor poetry. However, as James Gordon notes in his survey of Evangelical spirituality, these were exceptions, "offset by a vast output of devotional lyricism unique in Christian history. The hymns were the confessions of a redeemed sinner, the evangelistic tools of a gospel preacher..."[8] They were also deeply experiential. It may be the combination of the teaching (especially, perhaps, the Revival emphasis on "new birth") and the concern for Christian experience that explains their enduring nature.

Perhaps the single most significant feature of the Wesleys' poetry was the proclamation of the new birth. Conversion and the need for it was a distinctive characteristic of Revival spirituality. It is therefore no surprise to find this expressed in the hymnody. J. R. Watson puts it thus: "'Change my nature' is a phrase at the centre of Charles Wesley's evangelical hymnody."[9] This is what the Lord's people were to sing about. This same feature was equally reflected in the more

Calvinist tradition of Watts, Newton and Cowper. The hymnody of the nineteenth century tended to be a contest over orthodoxy. The hymns of the eighteenth-century were closer both chronologically and spiritually to the Revival itself, and hence although not exempt from polemic, tended to reflect the themes of revival and new birth.

Two examples from Charles Wesley's corpus will illustrate the point. In his great hymn of the new birth, "And Can it Be", written in 1738, he emphasized a wide range of spiritual points, from the cross to assurance. The fourth stanza read as follows:

> *Long my imprisoned spirit lay,*
> *fast bound in sin and nature's night;*
> *thine eye diffused a quickening ray;*
> *I woke, the dungeon flamed with light;*
> *my chains fell off, my heart was free,*
> *I rose, went forth, and followed thee.*

The poetry was classic Evangelical spirituality. The human soul was held captive by sin; the miraculous intervention of God brought light into darkness; and then, of course, the captured soul was released, the chains fell off, the heart of the believer was set free and the disciple commenced the life-journey of following Christ. The metaphor was a powerful one and has remained so. The same emphasis was also seen in one of Charles Wesley's great nativity hymns:

> *Mild He lays His glory by,*
> *Born — that man no more may die,*
> *Born — to raise the sons of earth,*
> *Born — to give them second birth.*[10]

Again, a helpful combination of theological themes was present. Kenosis (that is, self-emptying), incarnation and atonement all feature. The reader was, however, left in no doubt as to the purpose which lay behind the incarnation – redemption and second birth. As Newport and Campbell comment, it reflected "the traditional evangelical view of the redemptive act as greater than the spiritual act."[11] In other words, Jesus was born in order to die. Such a shame we sing it today only at Christmas!

The theme of new birth featured in other hymns by Wesley (e.g. "He breaks the power of cancelled sin, he sets the prisoner free"; "New life the dead receive" and "Jesus! the name to sinners dear, the name to sinners given"). The theme is present in other writers but most prominent in Wesley; once we move into the hymns of Newton and Cowper we encounter other classic themes of the spiritual armoury of early Evangelicalism – most notably that of grace.

The contested area in early Evangelical hymnody was principally that of the nature of redemption in Christ. In short, was the atonement for all (Wesley) or limited to the elect (Whitefield, Newton)? Spiritually, Evangelicals came to affirm both truths, but the conflict not only resulted in personal animosity between the Wesleys and Whitefield but was played out particularly in their hymnody.

Wesley's hymns ring out with cries of the vastness and availability of God's grace and love. The examples are numerous. The theme is there both subtly and more overtly. From "And Can it Be" we sing, "so free, so infinite his grace", "and bled for Adam's helpless race" – that is, the atonement is for all. Similarly in the carol we know as "Hark the herald angels sing" – "light and life to all he brings, Risen with healing in his wings". Again, it is "to all", not only the elect. No exclusive Calvinism there! John Wesley's edition of hymns, mainly by Charles, originally published in 1780, with numerous editions since, also set out the issues openly, in what James Gordon called "a famous piece of devotional polemic"[12] – "For all my Lord was crucified, For all, for all, my Saviour died."[13] John added in another hymn, "that every fallen soul of man, may taste the grace that found out me."[14] The grace was free and for all – "'tis mercy all, immense and free", in the words of "And Can it Be".

The Calvinism which influenced Anglican Evangelicalism as well as much of traditional dissent gave an emphasis to grace which was much more centred on the eternal significance of the individual and the assurance of God's grace in the struggles of the Christian life. This stood in a degree of tension with the more Wesleyan emphases. We see this especially in the *Olney Hymnbook* and some of Newton's classic works. So, for example, "Amazing grace, how sweet the sound... I once was lost and now am found." Two stanzas in that hymn express this with clarity:

> *'Twas Grace that taught...*
> *my heart to fear.*
> *And Grace, my fears relieved.*
> *How precious did that Grace appear...*
> *the hour I first believed.*

> *Through many dangers, toils and snares...*
> *we have already come.*
> *'Twas Grace that brought us safe thus far...*
> *and Grace will lead us home.*[15]

Here are the classic themes of Puritan, Reformed

Evangelicalism – struggle against sin (not even a possible hint of Christian perfection this side of heaven), grace imparted into the heart of the individual, assurance of salvation and of the presence and guidance of God throughout the pilgrim's life. The same themes ring out from "Glorious things of thee are spoken":

> *God, whose word cannot be broken,*
> *formed thee for his own abode.*
> *On the Rock of Ages founded,*
> *what can shake thy sure repose?*

The Wesleyan doctrine of Christian perfection, articulated by John, was exclaimed and proclaimed in Charles's hymns. The problem was that Charles tended to use absolutes and superlatives in his descriptions that left the traditional spirituality of Evangelicalism feeling somewhat uneasy. So, the heart being all love, pure and spotless, praying without ceasing (see "Love divine"), all added to this sense that Wesley was at least suggesting the possibility of the perfect and sinless Christian life.

God's free grace for all, the possibility of Christian perfection, even hints at union with Christ – all pushed the boundaries of Protestant Evangelicalism, though remaining within them, and Wesley's great themes were firmly scriptural. The last stanza of "Love divine, all love's excelling", in which he had already written, "Let us all thy grace receive", is a good example with which to conclude our look at Wesley:

> *Finish then thy new creation,*
> *Pure and spotless let us be;*
> *Let us see thy great salvation,*

Perfectly restored in thee,
Changed from glory into glory,
Till in heaven we take our place,
Till we cast our crowns before thee,
Lost in wonder, love, and praise![16]

This is a wonderful song of praise, albeit with hints of perfectionism and the ultimate aim of intimate personal union with God, in whom we will indeed be "lost in wonder, love and praise!"

The hymnody of Romanticism and holiness

What happened to hymnody in the aftermath of the Revival?

The enthusiastic hymns of the Revival (in both Wesleyan and Calvinist traditions), the singing of the new birth and the grace of God, changed in nature as the eighteenth century entered the nineteenth, for a number of reasons.

First, hymn-singing moved not only from dissent and Methodism into Evangelical Anglicanism but also into the wider Established Church, with the official sanction given to the singing of hymns from 1820. (A court case brought in the Consistory Court of the Diocese of York in 1819 against the Revd Thomas Cotterill, an Evangelical vicar in Sheffield, ruled both hymns and psalms to be illegal, but their use was too widespread to stop.) Among those who embraced the opportunity with alacrity was the high church or Tractarian movement, which emerged from 1833 onwards. Hymns thus became vehicles for a much wider range of doctrine than previously. So, while it is certainly the case that nineteenth-century hymnody generally expounded orthodox Christian belief,[17] hymns also became vehicles for conveying ecclesiology and eucharistic doctrine which was highly suspect in Evangelical eyes.

Second, by around 1800, pipe organs had been introduced in the majority of town and city churches. As Hardy showed, there were still the vestiges of the "west gallery" tradition in rural areas. However, the days of the village band in the gallery playing a variety of instruments and tunes were ending.

Third, specific tunes now came to be associated with particular hymns. The effect of all of this was a greater degree of formality and control over the hymnody of the faithful.

Victorian Romanticism and its religious twin, the holiness movement, had a significant influence on hymnody. Romanticism's recovery of the values of idealism, sensuality, feeling and perfection influenced literature, philosophy, theology, culture and much else. In the Victorian period we see this outlook expressed in the idolization of childhood innocence, in the home, in Christmas traditions and inevitably in the hymnody of the period. A striking example was Mrs Cecil Frances Alexander (1818–95). She wrote most of her hymns before her marriage to a moderate Tractarian clergyman. She was brought up in Ireland in a more Evangelical culture. She was basically of orthodox conviction but did not emphasize conversion or evangelism.[18] The general influence of Victorian Romanticism and culture can be seen in the titles of some of her writings and hymns, many of which she wrote for children – for example, "All things bright and beautiful, all creatures great and small". Certainly, she had an idealized Romantic Victorian view of childhood: "Christian children all must be, Mild, obedient, good as He." The wider influence of Romanticism was seen in the final stanza of her "Once in royal David's city" – the rather bizarre, "Where like stars His children crowned, All in white shall wait around." She also wrote "There is a green hill far away", though the Romantic Victorian notion of a green hill was probably far removed from the realities of Golgotha. The point is that this wider influence of the Romantic tradition affected all hymnody.

Evangelical ministry was also affected through the influence of the holiness movement on hymnody. As we noted in Chapter 5, the characteristic mantra of holiness was surrender. The whole of life and being was given over to God. Christians' hearts and lives were to be consecrated to the Lord; they were to surrender everything to his devotion. Hymnody, which had become depersonalized, was once again made personal, even intimate. It was *my* heart and *my* life that was to be consecrated on the altar of God's praise. There was a renewed passion and intensity in this hymnody. On the more negative side, it once again left some believers worrying about "perfectionism" – in other words, the quest for "entire sanctification" left a number of doors wide open. These included debates over "second blessings", a loss of emphasis on the daily struggle of the Christian against sin, and an over-realized Romanticism (i.e. the worst examples lacked reality). The positives were, however, also significant and the change in the nature of hymnody had long-term effects into the contemporary era.

A classic example from this period was penned by Judson Van DeVenter:

All to Jesus, I surrender;
All to Him I freely give;
I will ever love and trust Him,
In His presence daily live, –
I surrender all, I surrender all,
All to Thee, my blessèd Savior, I surrender all.

By way of example closer to home we can consider Frances Ridley Havergal (1836–79) – many of the hymn-writers of this era were women. Frances herself presents something of a complicated picture. She rejected perfectionism and association with the holiness movement, wishing to retain her Calvinism. However, she also spoke of her full consecration and full surrender before the Lord, reflecting the general wider influence of the movement. She wrote of this in one of her hymns:

I am trusting Thee, Lord, Jesus,
Trusting only Thee;
Trusting Thee for full salvation,
Great and free.

The same theme can be seen in her autobiographical story:

I went for a little visit of five days [to Areley
House]. There were ten persons in the house, some
unconverted and long prayed for, some converted,
but not rejoicing Christians. He gave me the prayer,
Lord, give me all in this house! And He just did.
Before I left the house every one had got a blessing.
The last night of my visit after I had retired, the
governess asked me to go to the two daughters. They

*were crying, &c.; then and there both of them
trusted and rejoiced; it was nearly midnight. I was
too happy to sleep, and passed most of the night in
praise and renewal of my own consecration; and
these little couplets formed themselves, and chimed
in my heart one after another till they finished with
Ever, Only, ALL for Thee!*[19]

This, of course, was then reflected in her most famous
hymn:

*Take my life, and let it be
consecrated, Lord, to Thee.
Take my moments and my days;
let them flow in ceaseless praise.
Take my hands, and let them move
at the impulse of Thy love.
Take my feet, and let them be
swift and beautiful for Thee.
Take my voice, and let me sing
always, only, for my King.
Take my lips, and let them be
filled with messages from Thee.
Take my silver and my gold;
not a mite would I withhold.
Take my intellect, and use
every power as Thou shalt choose.
Take my will, and make it Thine;
it shall be no longer mine.
Take my heart, it is Thine own;
it shall be Thy royal throne.
Take my love, my Lord, I pour*

at Thy feet its treasure store.
Take myself, and I will be
ever, only, all for Thee.

Contemporary issues in the spirituality of hymnody

How can we make sense of this in our contemporary spirituality of song and hymnody? First, we need to understand the history. The contemporary emphasis on instrumental variety and a more folk-tune approach is actually a recovery of the earliest traditions of the Revival. Elements of the "west gallery" tradition are strongly reflected in modern Evangelical devotion. Both the "village band" and the "choir and organ" tradition which succeeded it also threw up questions over control and freedom, the role of singers, and the nature of the hymnody. We would do well to draw upon the heritage but not in an unthinking manner, aware of the pitfalls of the past.

Second, contemporary devotion through hymnody should draw upon the mighty strengths of the spiritual tradition. In the aftermath of the Revival the new hymnody's emphasis on doctrine and teaching, although used sometimes for polemical purposes, was a powerful tool for proclamation. Later Evangelicals (especially, though not exclusively, of the Anglican variety) came to realize that both sides of the truths of the Calvinist controversy (grace is sufficient for all − "immense and free"; and saving grace only for the elect of God − "how sweet the name of Jesus sounds in a believer's ear") needed to be believed, preached and sung. However, as we have seen, the strengths of the tradition also involve a personalization of faith and an emphasis on the consecrated Christian life.

Third, we need to appreciate the influences on the different genres that are sung in contemporary devotion. The classic strands of Puritanism and Calvinism mean that doctrinal poetry will carry significant weight. However, the influence of the holiness movement on modern Charismatic and neo-Pentecostal spirituality means that the emphasis here will be on personal surrender, union with Christ, the consecrated life, intimacy with God, and a more subjective approach.

These influences and expressions of hymnody are not incompatible. We need to express the whole range of these genres. However, what is crucial is that entertainment does not replace doctrine. Both in historical perspective and in contemporary practice we need to learn in both content and practice from our historical forebears. Doctrine, personal faith and the Christian life should all feature in devotional hymnody. Avoiding impersonal dryness on the one hand has to be balanced on the other against banality, reductionism and descent into mere amusement. Styles will and should vary, but we can ensure balance by singing the whole range of historical Evangelical hymnody, perhaps recovering something of the early emphases, not least on "new birth", and we can do so also in modern and contemporary hymn and song. "Amazing grace", "Love divine", "Here is love, vast as the ocean", "Take my life and let it be", can be sung happily alongside "How deep the Father's love for us", "Speak O Lord, as we come to you", "Before the throne of God above" and the vast range of spiritual songs and choruses that now grace many church worship services. The Evangelical spiritual and devotional tradition is rich and deep in its hymnody.

Notes

....

1. Ian Bradley, *Abide With Me*, London: SCM Press, 1997, pp. 9–10.
2. G. Mursell, *English Spirituality, From Earliest Times to 1700*, London: SPCK, 2008, p. 97; Kenneth G. C. Newport and Ted A. Campbell (eds), *Charles Wesley: Life, Literature and Legacy*, Peterborough: Epworth, 2007, p. 405; James Gordon, *Evangelical Spirituality*, London: SPCK, 1991, p. 16.
3. The name given to followers of the Oxford Movement, led by John Henry Newman, which published the "Tracts for the Times" (hence the name Tractarians) arguing for a more Catholic understanding of the Anglican Church and its authority, ministry and sacraments.
4. Thomas Hardy, *Under the Greenwood Tree* (first published 1872), Middlesex: Penguin English Library, 1978, p. 33.
5. Mursell, *English Spirituality*, p. 61.
6. Mursell, *English Spirituality*, p. 63.
7. Mursell, *English Spirituality*, p. 97; see also Gordon, *Evangelical Spirituality*, p. 16.
8. Gordon, *Evangelical Spirituality*, pp. 16–17.
9. J. R. Watson, "The Hymns of Charles Wesley and the Poetic Tradition", in Newport and Campbell (eds), *Wesley*, p. 366.
10. Mursell, *English Spirituality*, p. 99.
11. Newport and Campbell, *Wesley*, p. 371.
12. Gordon, *Evangelical Spirituality*, p. 26.
13. Gordon, *Evangelical Spirituality*, p. 26, quoting John Wesley, *A Collection of Hymns for the Use of the People Called Methodists*, first published 1780. The quote is from Hymn 34.
14. John Wesley, *Collection of Hymns*, Hymn 33.
15. *Olney Hymnbook*, London, 1779, facsimile copy of the original, Cowper and Newton Museum, Olney, 1979.
16. John Wesley, *Collection of Hymns*, Hymn 385.
17. Bradley, *Abide With Me*, p. 110.
18. Bradley, *Abide With Me*, pp. 94–95.
19. Taken from W. J. Limmer Shepherd, *Great Hymns and their Stories*, Cambridge: Lutterworth Press, revised edition, 1980.

7

Revival and Revivalism

....

P ray to the Lord that the Revivals and Awakenings of
the mid eighteenth century might be repeated.

The Revival drove evangelism significantly higher
up the agenda of the Evangelical pioneers. Although the
first missionary societies were in place prior to the Revival,
there was a significant impetus subsequently, with both
denominational and inter-denominational societies taking
the call for new birth to new places. The Lord had moved
over the land and would surely do so again. The Revival in
England was, of course, part of a wider pattern of revival
in the eighteenth century across the English-speaking world.
Since then, also, there have been numerous revivals in various
places in the UK, often within certain geographical bounds
(e.g. the Welsh Revival of 1904–5), but also much further
afield, fuelled by missionary enterprise.

What if the Lord needed a helping hand? In that case
it was the duty of the Lord's people to supply the necessary
assistance. So for the decades, indeed centuries, after the
great Revival we moved into the era of means, programmes,
events, campaigns and great evangelists from D. L. Moody
to Billy Graham. To understand the history and why these
matters generated controversy (then and now) will help us
in understanding the different approaches to revival and
evangelism today.

Some draw a very sharp, almost certainly too severe, distinction between revival and revivalism. So Iain Murray sees a clear difference between "religious excitements" and "authentic spiritual awakening".[1] The reality is considerably more complex. There was genuine debate within the Evangelical movement over the appropriateness of "means" – that is, human programmes to encourage, or induce, revival. Moody, as we will see, was a case in point. He was an evangelist of historic significance, deeply influenced by the holiness movement, employing many of the methods associated with revivalism, and mostly remaining in the mainstream. Not all did so.

Revival

Revival was bound by neither class nor geography. Whitefield and Wesley preached to crowds of tens of thousands. The places where they preached included, famously, the Kingswood district of Bristol (where the miners turned out to hear them), Moorfields (later the site of Whitefield's tabernacle) and Kennington in London. They spoke to the aristocracy and the poor, in Cornwall, Yorkshire and Scotland. There were localized revivals and both the church and the nation were changed. Wesley travelled, it is estimated, over 200,000 miles on horseback in the course of his long ministry.

The 1730s saw revival in both Britain and North America. The year 1735 saw the conversion of Howell Harris and Daniel Rowland, who began an itinerant ministry in Wales, and also the conversion of George Whitefield. He stirred London and Bristol, and his conversion was followed by those of John and Charles Wesley in 1738. The mid 1730s also saw the outbreak of revival in Massachusetts under the ministry of Jonathan Edwards. The story continued into the following decades.[2]

Large crowds, itinerant preaching, the new birth, conviction of sin – all of these were characteristic of the outbreak of revival. However, the question may rightly be asked, "What is revival?" Evangelicals give great weight to revival in terms of both the heritage and contemporary practice. Revival is prayed for and worked for, but to understand what this means today we must first reflect upon its characteristics.

In 1737 Jonathan Edwards' "faithful narrative" was published in England. The full title was *A Faithful Narrative of a Surprizing Work of God in the conversion of many hundred souls*. It was Edwards' description and assessment of the outbreak of revival in the town of Northampton in Massachusetts, New England and the surrounding area in the years 1733–35. Isaac Watts and John Guyse wrote the introduction to the English edition. They placed the actual local events into wider context, describing the outbreaks as "a special occasion to manifest the divinity of this gospel by a plentiful effusion of his Spirit where it is preached: then sinners are turned into saints in numbers…"[3]

This may reasonably act as a working definition for revival. Such an event is extraordinary, involves the outpouring of the Spirit, the preaching of the gospel and widespread conversion. Edwards, in his own writing, remarked upon the suddenness of conversion, the increasing number of conversions, the ever-increasing awareness of sinfulness and the fruit of love, joy and praise of God. The effect reached all ages and classes of society. There was thus "a general awakening". Edwards placed great weight upon the growing awareness of conviction of sin, understanding of God's wrath and (in classic Calvinist terms) of the consequences. He refers to "a remarkable communication of the Spirit of God... at special seasons of mercy".[4] Thomas Kidd notes the emphasis in early American Evangelicalism of "dramatically increased emphases on *seasons of revival*, or *outpourings of the Holy Spirit*, and on *converted sinners experiencing God's love personally*."[5]

Whitefield also described the work which God had brought about as "amazing" and observed that God had been doing marvellous things.[6] While in North Carolina he talked of his hope for "more plentiful effusions of God's Spirit in these parts."[7] Wesley also mentioned the speed with which revival came, and that many sinners were saved. He added, "This I term a *great work of God*; so great as I have not read of for several ages."[8]

Mark Noll has noted that the revivals of the mid 1730s were not altogether new, but were unusual.[9] They clearly involved something unexpected – powerful preaching of the new birth and increased conviction of sin. The unexpected and unusual nature of the revivals emphasized the sovereignty of God rather than diminishing it.

Spiritually, revival is central to Evangelical piety. Evangelical believers look and pray for revival to come. At different times and depending upon the differing spiritual heritage, believers have placed different weight upon dependency on God for a special outpouring of the Spirit and the use of human means in order to encourage the circumstances of revival. In either case the spiritual importance of revival historically is that it encourages evangelism in the contemporary life of Evangelical believers.

Edwards reported also the side-effects: laughter, tears (which he describes as like a flood), weeping – indeed, loud weeping. The cause of distress was that God in his sovereignty might not have mercy upon a sinner; the joy was the delight that he did so. The experiences of Wesley and Whitefield were similar. These phenomena themselves did not confirm that this was a work of the Spirit, but neither did they mean that the Spirit was not present. Both Wesley and Whitefield were rather sceptical about the occurrences, the latter more so. The authentic nature of revival, however, was measured by conviction of sin, conversion and the consequent fruitfulness of the Christian life.

There were also other factors at work. Edwards did not dismiss the impact of long-term effective pastoral ministry. Although he had only been the minister of Northampton, Massachusetts for five years when revival came, he had succeeded his grandfather. The area was also semi-rural, a region of small towns. It was not frontier land but had settled communities. The impact was significant, with Edwards reporting some 600 conversions.

The result of revival was, not unnaturally, to seek more of God's outpouring of the Spirit. More emphasis came to be given to human means and programmes, so that revival became, perhaps, a slightly less surprising work of God. Much of this remained within the mainstream of Evangelical faith, though some expressions of revival stretched the boundaries considerably.

Revivalism

On a craggy hillside in Staffordshire the Methodist dissidents gathered. It had rained in the morning, but the sky had cleared on this day in May 1806. Some local preachers gathered with the crowd; there was singing, prayer for the Spirit, and short, sharp preaching addressed to the heart. This first camp meeting, on Mow Cop, marked the growing influence in certain areas of revivalism within the now rather more formalized Methodist tradition. Those who had been the radical enthusiasts of the 1740s had now become the conservative boundary keepers of Methodism. This was the beginning of what became known as Primitive Methodism – rather strange terminology, but designed to emphasize that the intent was to keep Methodism close to its original roots.

The Methodist radicals had been influenced by events in North America. The "camp meeting" was essentially imported from North America, through the visits of Lorenzo Dow who met dissident Methodists in the north-west of England. Dow's republicanism, alongside the dissidents' revivalism, with its disorder bordering on chaos, horrified the conservative Methodist establishment. The North of England, Cornwall and Wales were the main areas of influence – geographically and culturally distant from the mainstream of the movement. A future Methodist leader, Jabez Bunting, denounced what he called the "rant and extravagancies" of the revivalists.[10]

So, it was Lorenzo Dow who persuaded Hugh Bourne, a local revivalist leader on the Staffordshire/Cheshire border, to inaugurate the first English camp meeting. The day-long event on Mow Cop on 31 May 1806 was attended by some 2,000–4,000 people. A second meeting followed in July and lasted three days, with some sixty conversions. A third followed in August at Norton-in-the-Moors. Bourne defied the Methodist Conference, held a meeting on the Wrekin in 1808 (mountains, lakes and rivers are always attractive to revivalism under the influence of the wider Romantic movement) and claimed to be simply continuing John Wesley's field preaching.

Bourne was expelled from the Methodist Conference. Nevertheless, the Primitive Methodists slowly emerged and were gradually joined by other dissident groups. In time they expanded their influence, not least in the Midlands and the North of England. They had particular appeal to the working industrial classes, with their rather radical local and anti-hierarchical message, the enthusiasm of the camp meetings and the somewhat chaotic worship (in contrast to the more formal, even liturgical practices of Wesley, though there was much greater divergence after his death), and there were a number of local revivals. The Primitive Methodists acquired the nickname "ranters". Innovations such as women preachers fared much better among the various Methodist secessionist groups (of which the Primitive Methodists were just one example). By 1830 the Primitive Methodists had around 35,000 members; the Wesleyans some 232,000. So, although small, the Primitive Methodist movement was not insignificant,[11] and in the following decades its growth rate was greater than that of the parent body.[12]

On the other side of the Atlantic revival broke out in Logan County, Kentucky, gathering pace by 1799. The focus was on the traditional "communion season", with the celebration of the Lord's Supper marked by intense spiritual preparation and preaching. As news of revival spread, crowds arrived and camped nearby. Thus began the idea of camp meetings. On 8 August 1801 at Cane Ridge, Kentucky, for the best part of a week, somewhere between 12,000 and 25,000 people gathered on a hillside. There were numerous preaching stands set up among the crowds. Wolffe comments that "the multitude joined in a cacophony of singing, praying, wailing and ecstatic acclamation."[13] As was so often the case with revivalism, the lack of order – social as well as ecclesiastical – challenged the establishment – both social and ecclesiastical. Camp meetings and their associated revivalism and revival spread over the southern part of the USA. Thousands attended camp meetings – the beginnings, perhaps, of mass revivalist movements.

The leadership of the established denominations reacted with some disdain. The camp-meeting phenomenon was essentially rural. It was particularly strong among the Methodists and the Baptists – those perhaps least restrained by the traditional Calvinism of the Presbyterians. By the 1830s, the era of the ministry of Charles Finney, the camp meetings did become, as ever, somewhat more institutionalized, with more permanent campsites. The standard features, however, were still present – hymns, prayer, exhortation, a mourners' bench and much emotionalism.

Charles Finney (1792–1875) was a controversial American revivalist. His view was that in order to ensure revival, "new measures" were needed. Traditional Calvinists were appalled; Finney rejected Calvinism with some vigour. The "new measures" included evangelistic campaigns and events, and the development of an "anxious bench" where enquirers could be counselled and prayed for. Some of these measures, although developed over time, have become the norm in Evangelical evangelism. The anxious bench became the enquirers' room under Moody and the follow-up counsellor under Graham.

Charles Grandison Finney was born on 29 August 1792 and worked as a teacher and then a lawyer. He experienced a classic conversion in 1821 and then the second blessing – the baptism of the Holy Spirit which, according to Wolffe, he described as "like a wave of electricity".[14] Finney, unlike the later, and more theologically balanced Moody, appealed to the professional classes with his legal training and logical thought, but was also given to melodramatic description – John Wolffe notes his "vivid evocation of the smoke of the torment of sinners in hell".[15]

Finney is famous for his advocacy of the so-called "new measures". By 1825–26 he was leading revival ministry in western New York state. He was not alone; the social and cultural setting made the area susceptible to new religious movements and there were a number to choose from. So what were these methodological innovations initiated by Finney? Itinerant preaching, preaching for revival in a direct, even theatrical manner, sustained periods of prayer, the "anxious bench", protracted meetings, experimentation and emotionalism were the hallmarks. Not all the "new measures" were new, and it is clear from the list that there was a careful interplay of spirituality and method. Discerning between the two is a crucial element of mature Evangelical spirituality in relation to revival.

The main criticism levelled at Finney was the victory of method over content, style over substance, but there were also theological concerns. The question was, once again, what was the role of human agency in the proclamation of new birth and the conversion process? Finney led a series of revival campaigns in the late 1820s and early 1830s. The anxious bench or seat kept up the emotional momentum. In the revival in Rochester, NY, Finney himself noted that charges of fanaticism had become fewer, while many of the more influential classes had responded. In 1832 he accepted the pastorate of Chatham Street Chapel in New York City, illustrating his own movement into a more settled form of ministry. His *Lectures on Revivals of Religion* (1835) were built on the premise of human agency in revival. The adoption of the "new measures" was an implicit rejection of Calvinism. Finney's work moved the "camp meeting" revivalism into a new era and a new focus; this did not, however, entirely supersede the earlier revivalism.

Finney did not visit England until 1849–51. He had a modest impact, unlike Moody, just a couple of decades later.

Moody and Sankey

David Bebbington describes Dwight Lyman Moody (1837–99) and Ira David Sankey (1840–1908) as like Marks and Spencer; that is, they are inextricably linked, at least in the Evangelical mind. Elsewhere he describes Moody as an "outstanding figure".[16] The fact that many contemporary Evangelicals have never heard of either of them simply illustrates the paucity of teaching on Evangelical history.

Both critics and adorers agree on Moody's influence. He had no significant education and was not ordained. Many myths have grown up around him, but he was neither a Pentecostal before the Pentecostals nor, in his ministry, did method triumph over message. Many of his emphases have been carried through into the mainstream of Evangelicalism. He was influenced, of course, by many of the developments we have considered so far, and some of his methods were carried forward in more openly revivalist ways, but Bebbington has the correct assessment:

*A stress on avoiding worldliness, together
with a gospel neutral between Calvinism and
Arminianism, a mild tone and premillennial
teaching were to become the orthodoxy of
conservative Evangelicalism in the earlier twentieth
century. Moody, as much as any individual, was its
creator.*[17]

Moody was born in 1837 in Northfield, Massachusetts, close
to Edwards' country, which had by now become influenced
by Unitarianism. He worked as a cobbler and was converted
in Boston in 1855. Two years later he headed to Chicago
to sell shoes. He was active in the revival in Chicago in
1857, worked for the YMCA and served as the founding
pastor of Illinois Street Church from 1864. Moody's lack of
both formal education and denominational ordination did
nothing to damage his effectiveness.

A date for Moody to remember was 8 October 1871. It
was neither the date of his birth, nor even of his new birth.
Rather, it was the date of the great fire that devastated old
Chicago, which was largely built of wood. With it went all of
Moody's classic activist ministry. Some 300 people died and
100,000 were made homeless. The Illinois Street Church
was gone. So was the YMCA building (Moody was by now
the YMCA's President) and its Farwell Hall where Moody
was a regular preacher. However, the effect of the fire was
to free him from the multifarious occupations that had
characterized his ministry. He now urged attention to two
things – consecrating one's life to God, and concentrating on
one key thing, which for him was to be winning souls. He had
already formed his partnership with Ira D. Sankey, who sang
spiritual and sacred songs at Moody's events. He was now

invited to visit Britain once again, which he did for two years, from 1873 to 1875.

Moody had first visited England in 1867. It was during this visit that he became acquainted with Charles Haddon Spurgeon and became an ardent admirer of the great Baptist preacher. He was also drawn into the circle of the nascent Christian holiness movement through the Mildmay Conferences under the auspices of William Pennefather of St Jude's, Mildmay Park. In 1872 Moody spoke from the Mildmay platform, and Pennefather was one of the originators of the invitation to Moody for his 1873–75 mission. After the Chicago fire, with his diary cleared and with his heart also clearing, and influenced by Keswick, Moody sought the renewed empowerment of the Holy Spirit. The spiritual refreshment which this brought flooded into his soul while he sought to raise funds in New York for fire relief in Chicago. He referred to this as receiving power for service; this language of empowerment was Keswick holiness language. Although there are clearly some links of language between this expression and later Pentecostalism and neo-Pentecostalism, there was no tongues-speaking as evidence of Spirit-baptism (the classic Pentecostal position). This again was a reflection of Moody's moderate premillennial dispensationalism (that is, a belief in the imminent return of Christ to inaugurate the thousand years of peace and blessedness, but without undue obsession with signs of the times or the fixing of specific dates).

In all, Moody visited Britain six times. In 1873–75 he travelled around the great cities of Britain preaching the gospel, accompanied by Sankey and his music and song. It culminated in the period March–June 1875 when he was preaching to around 12,000 people per night in Islington, and perhaps as many as two and a half million in total.[18] The British Evangelical leader, the Earl of Shaftesbury, was sceptical about the methods employed by Moody, but decided he should attend one of the meetings to find out for himself. Afterwards Shaftesbury revised his opinion. He declared himself impressed by Moody's humility, the simplicity of his message and the effect on ordinary people. Interestingly, their eschatology was very similar. They were both motivated by the second coming of Christ but eschewed all the grisly detail of Evangelical schemes, which set out precise schedules of the events of the end times matched to the contemporary signs, with dates specified and interpretations of the numerology of the Bible that would leave mathematicians mystified!

One of the consequences of Moody's British campaigns was that hundreds of workers, especially women, were generated for Shaftesbury's beloved Evangelical societies.[19] Bebbington notes that "the legacy of his Glasgow mission included free morning breakfasts for down-and-outs, free Sunday dinners for destitute children and an orphanage by the sea."[20] Moody was a layman and, like Shaftesbury, he believed that it was the laity, male and female, who were to be God's evangelists.

One of the points of contention in Moody's work was his methodology. His events were well planned and advertised, preceded by door-to-door visitation. He put together an organization to manage the programme of activities. It was the beginning of the mass evangelistic campaign, which some viewed as over-reliant on human means. Certainly, his campaigns hardly demonstrated the historic spontaneity of the Spirit.

He instituted an enquirers' room for prayer and offered

counsel to those who made commitments. The second Great Awakening had seen the use of the "mourners' bench", and Finney had used the "anxious seat". Moody extended this, but his concern was not public show, but private certainty of the genuineness of conversion. Dignitaries, invited by Moody, would sit on the platform at his meetings – exactly the sort of thing that Evangelicals a generation earlier had so strongly resisted.

The most innovative element to Moody's campaigns was the use of music and song, not least through his partnership with Sankey. Their events were effectively marketed on the model of the music hall. From half an hour before proceedings began there was congregational singing and, of course, Sankey's powerful solos during the meeting itself. They became known as "revival meetings" and Sankey's contribution as "the singing Gospel".

The approach was businesslike – Moody was well trained in business self-sufficiency. Business financed the campaigns, in some places in the United States constructing auditoriums or other buildings for the meetings. Moody worked with the local churches, gaining the support of the pastors and organizing prayer meetings and support for the campaigns. He avoided conflicts with church programmes and events. The revival movement, however, had developed beyond contained rural outbreaks, and was now faced with the need to evangelize the new large conurbations. It was an evangelistic challenge that burdened many in the nineteenth century and some of Moody's methodological approaches can be explained by the requirement to reach larger audiences in the big cities. However, the danger was one of human-induced revival, with time and place selected, and the organization set up in advance – scarcely an outpouring of the Spirit.

Theologically, Moody was the archetypical Evangelical.[21] He preached from the Bible, emphasizing the cross and conversion – the need for new birth. He preached on the new birth 184 times between 1881 and 1899.[22] His methodology was to seek out Bible passages related to his themes and preach through them. He resisted building sermons on single verses. There was an essential simplicity: Moody never forgot that the salvation of souls was his driving force.

Moody was not preserved from the Calvinist/Arminian controversy. Strict Calvinists accused him of preaching the Arminian message that all could be saved through the gospel. With his message of salvation and his carefully planned methods, the source of this criticism is easy to see. In reality though, Moody reflected the moderate Calvinism which predominated among Evangelicals in England's Established Church. He was close to Spurgeon (hardly an Arminian) and adopted most of the Calvinist positions. He did so, however, with a degree of caution. Bebbington notes that Moody remarked, "I don't try to reconcile God's sovereignty with man's free agency."[23] This combination of God's initiative and human response was one of the most powerful messages of the spirituality of the Evangelical Revival, and it has been carried forward into contemporary life and practice.

Moody returned to live in Northfield in the late 1870s and established the Northfield Conferences where he passed on the Keswick teaching on holiness that had affected him so deeply. Indeed, Keswick speakers came to Northfield. Moody himself appeared on the platform at Keswick in 1892. His style and temperament were well suited to the Romanticism of the age – emotion and will were emphasized over reason, as reflected in the holiness teaching. This was demonstrated also in his premillennialism, with an emotional attachment to the belief that the imminent return of Christ would correct all things that were amiss in the world. He cautioned against an excessive emphasis on instant and entire sanctification, as indeed did the Keswick movement itself. Despite his own only very basic education, among his many legacies was his training school – subsequently, of course, called the Moody Bible Institute.

Moody's legacy comes from his inspiration, his well-grounded theology, his passion for souls and his adaptation of mass evangelism to the urban environment.

The spirituality of contemporary evangelism

The impact of all of this upon contemporary Evangelical spirituality is this: certain key characteristics of revival lie at the heart of the spiritual endeavour of the Evangelical. These can perhaps best be summarized as: the sovereignty of God in revival; the preaching of the new birth; and the conviction of sin. There would also be some weight given to the means of revival, which should not be dismissed as "mere revivalism", including prayer for revival and the use of appropriate means in mass evangelism.

There remain some areas of caution, including concern about excessive weight being given to accompanying phenomena, caution about over-emphasis on human means, and a desire for the effectiveness of revival to be judged by its fruit.

Although differing parts of the Evangelical tradition may give varying weight to different aspects of revival, the importance of the phenomenon of revival and its utter dependency upon the sovereignty of God lie at the spiritual heart of Evangelicalism.

Notes

1. Timothy George (ed.), *Mr Moody and the Evangelical Tradition*, London and New York: Continuum, 2004, p. 93; Iain Murray, *Revival and Revivalism*, Edinburgh: Banner of Truth Trust, 1994, p. xix.
2. For the full story see Richard Turnbull, *Reviving the Heart: The Story of the Eighteenth Century Revival*, Oxford: Lion, 2012.
3. Jonathan Edwards, *A Narrative of Surprising Conversions*, in *Jonathan Edwards on Revival*, Edinburgh: Banner of Truth Trust, 1991 edition, p. 2.
4. Murray, *Revival and Revivalism*, p. 20.
5. Thomas S. Kidd, *The Great Awakening*, New Haven: Yale University Press, 2007, p. xiv.
6. D. Bruce Hindmarsh, *The Evangelical Conversion Narrative*, Oxford: OUP, 2005, p. 63.
7. Kidd, *Great Awakening*, p. 52.
8. Hindmarsh, *Conversion Narrative*, p. 63.
9. Mark Noll, *The Rise of Evangelicalism*, Leicester: Apollos, 2004, p. 69.
10. John Wolffe, *The Expansion of Evangelicalism*, Leicester: IVP, 2006, p. 61.
11. Wolffe, *Expansion*, p. 77.
12. Wolffe, *Expansion*, p. 82.
13. Wolffe, *Expansion*, pp. 55–56.
14. Wolffe, *Expansion*, p. 70.
15. Wolffe, *Expansion*, p. 111.
16. David Bebbington, *The Dominance of Evangelicalism*, Leicester: IVP, 2005, p. 42.
17. George, *Mr Moody*, p. 85.
18. George, *Mr Moody*, p. 79.
19. Richard Turnbull, *Shaftesbury: The Great Reformer*, Oxford: Lion, 2010, pp. 200, 209.
20. Bebbington, *Dominance*, p. 44.

21. George, *Mr Moody*, p. 75.
22. Bebbington, *Dominance*, p. 43.
23. George, *Mr Moody*, p. 83.

8

Issues in Contemporary Evangelical Spirituality

....

The challenge of a coherent, effective and powerful spirituality is ever more acute for Evangelicalism. Increasing fragmentation, loss of historic memory and secular advance have led to a spiritual crisis. A significant part of Evangelicalism relies upon spiritual practices imported from elsewhere and much of what passes for Evangelical spirituality is shockingly shallow.

We have seen two things in our review of Evangelical history, personality and practice. First, Evangelical spirituality, like Evangelicalism itself, is not monolithic. Due to the various historical influences we have considered, we can see why there are different emphases and indeed various practices within the Evangelical spiritual tradition. Second, we would also assert that Evangelicalism provides spiritual depth, transformative values and a passion for evangelism and service. The movement has produced some extraordinary figures for Christ.

It remains for us in this chapter to review Evangelical unity and diversity, and the challenges faced by Evangelical spirituality. Perhaps, most importantly, we should consider a vision for the spiritual renewal of the movement.

Unity and diversity in spirituality

An appreciation of unity and diversity within Evangelical spirituality helps us in recognizing appropriate diversity of life and practice. To comprehend this framework ensures that the central aims and vitality of Evangelical spirituality are maintained. The approach enables a wise discernment of spiritual practices which enable us to assess what belongs to the core and what crosses the boundaries of what could be properly described as Evangelicalism.

How then can we formulate an approach?

1. Recognizing diversity within biblical, historic and doctrinal boundaries

Diversity is not necessarily a good thing in its own right. The post-modern quest for diversity carries significant weaknesses as well as strengths. From a spiritual point of view, not all spiritual practices are healthy or biblical. The framework we noted in Chapter 1 grounds Evangelical spirituality within the boundaries of the Word of God and the cross of Christ. Our investigations have shown that there is an appropriate and healthy diversity across the range of the Evangelical tradition, but that there are also boundaries. Where do those boundaries lie? An authentically Evangelical spirituality will be shaped by an open and humble submission to Scripture (practice must be biblical), an awareness of the historic tradition (precedents are important), discipleship which is transformative (there must be fruit), a reticence about spiritual practices from elsewhere, and a caution about an over-realized view of God's action in the world. A mature Evangelical spirituality will be aware of both unity within appropriate diversity and the spiritual limits of that unity.

2. Embracing the object of spiritual practices rather than investing meaning in the practices themselves

Evangelicals will wish to embrace a number of spiritual practices which have grown out of Evangelical history. These would include, for example, both the place of emotion, and the advocacy of revival. However, responsible Evangelical spirituality will wish to avoid emotionalism and revivalism – in other words, when the particular spiritual emphases or practices themselves move centre stage and replace the Word and the cross as the central focal points of Evangelical spirituality. When a practice comes to carry meaning in itself, then it has probably crossed over the boundary of what can be regarded as a mainstream Evangelical spiritual discipline. We will consider some examples below.

3. Recognizing the distinction between the normative and the exceptional

A constant tension in understanding the spiritual tradition has been that of expectation and anticipation. To what extent can Evangelicals *expect* a contemporary replication of the ministry and practices of Jesus, and to what degree should Evangelicals *anticipate* the new heaven and the new earth? Evangelicalism has generally adopted a cautious approach in this area, although this has been challenged in some areas of contemporary Evangelical spirituality. Essentially the approach has been that the direct copying of the actions of Jesus and the other practices of the New Testament into ministry today should be seen as exceptional rather than normative. This is also the case with the realization, or the breaking in, of the future kingdom into the present. These things are seen as a reality but not the normative pattern of ministry.

Case study: assessing the emerging church movement

The emerging church movement is an approach to spiritual life and practice which seeks particularly to relate to post-modern culture. As such it embraces a very wide range of approaches to spirituality and will tend to resist characterization as Evangelical, although sometimes alternative labels such as "post-Evangelical" might be used. This is not the place for a full reflection on emerging church in its various aspects, but spiritually it transcends the Charismatic/Pietist part of our framework and hence gives us some insight into what does and does not constitute Evangelical spirituality. The characteristics of the emerging church movement may be described as follows:

- Values are more central than doctrine.

- Participation is more communal than individual.

- Spirituality and worship are more mystical (emphasizing the mystery elements of the faith, even to excess) and varied than in mainstream Evangelicalism.

- Boundaries are more porous than defined.

- Transformation is prioritized over evangelism.

Some of the emphases and practices adopted by the emerging church movement are those which can find an honoured place within Evangelical spirituality – for example, the desire to reach the outsider and to model counter-cultural Christian values. Others, however, place the movement outside of the Evangelical framework. Some elements of the spirituality of the movement will be particularly attractive to those within the more Charismatic part of the Evangelical framework. This will include the emphasis on the mystical in worship, and wider approaches to alternative worship (perhaps emphasizing the sensual, the use of the body, art, etc.), including more weight being given to the Eucharist, and the use of incense, symbolism and movement. Spiritually, the movement transcends the classic divisions not only between denominations but between faiths.

Emerging church participants will place significant stress upon values – love, transformation – rather than traditional doctrines – some of which (e.g. the nature and existence of hell) may be explicitly denied. To some degree this is due to the desire to make the boundaries more porous and less defined so as to attract to Christianity those who might not otherwise seek to explore the meaning of faith. Hence there is appeal to the spiritual, the mystical and the communal.

From the point of view of spirituality, the main question Evangelicals will wish to raise is that of the relationship of spirituality to doctrine. Using the framework we have established, mainstream Evangelical spirituality, for all its variety, will wish to ensure that spiritual life and practice remain firmly within the established biblical, doctrinal and historical framework. Those Evangelical Christians whose spiritual practices are themselves entirely within the mainstream, but who are attracted by the emphasis on spirituality, mysticism and community, will need to take particular care to ensure that practice remains rooted in biblical doctrine. Evangelical spirituality does have boundaries; spiritually, it is conversion that moves an individual across that boundary into faith, not mystical experience.

Challenges to Evangelical spirituality

The exploration of unity and diversity, together with the reflection on emerging church, begins to reveal something of the challenges facing Evangelical spirituality. Indeed, it is the combination of the two words "Evangelical" and "spirituality" that poses the challenge. In the age in which we live, if "spirituality" has increasing attraction and meaning, then "Evangelical" has become less appealing. If all the weight is placed upon "spirituality" as distinct from "Evangelical", there is considerable danger of spiritual practice being evacuated of content and meaning, at least within the Evangelical tradition. What then are the challenges to the development of a distinctively Evangelical spirituality?

Secularization and loss of historic memory

The effect of secularization on Evangelical spirituality is significant; the impact of the loss of historic memory is profound. The shift in cultural worldview which has taken place in the last 200 years is dramatic. A number of important assumptions are now challenged.

The first of these is the relationship of Christ and culture. An increasingly secular culture has led to many Christians conforming or adapting their worldview to the contemporary secular culture. As well as being contrary to the biblical teaching of Romans 12, the effect of this is to move that which is central to Christian faith (and Evangelical Christian faith) to the margin, and move that which is on the margin to the centre. In other words, distinctively Christian views tend to be played down and anything which emphasizes cultural accessibility is elevated in the interests of engagement.

Second, secularization has quite simply led to a lower

155

level of Bible insight and knowledge not only among the wider community but also among Christians. Hence there is something of a loss of confidence in the revelation of God, the purposes of God and even the prospects of God; will God actually survive to act in the ways Evangelical Christians have always proclaimed? Spirituality is seen as a means of engagement with the contemporary age (reaching out to the mystical, the inner self, the numinous, the sensual, the creative and so on). In the case of the loss of confidence in the biblical revelation, the consequence is that the spiritual engagement with the age becomes divorced from the content of the revelation in Scripture.

Evangelical spirituality is biblical, doctrinal and historic. A full appreciation of the dynamism and power of the Evangelical spiritual tradition is not possible without an acute awareness of its history. That has been the task, at least in part, of this book. History provides context, insight and inspiration. Our history reminds us of the power of Evangelical conversion, the centrality of Scripture, the transforming role of the Spirit and the place of faith in the public square. History gives us insight into the breadth and the limits of Evangelical spirituality. We would do well to pay more heed to our history.

The future of the Charismatic movement

The future of the Charismatic movement is critical for the future of Evangelical Christianity. This statement is true both positively and negatively. The influence of neo-Pentecostalism as expressed both within and without the historic denominations has brought countless benefits. This particular strand of the spiritual tradition has emphasized that Evangelical faith is an emotional as well as an intellectual faith and that this can and should be expressed in our spirituality, from hymnody to evangelism and social transformation.

However, the Charismatic tradition will also have a significant impact upon the future of Evangelicalism for negative reasons. If neo-Pentecostalism loses its historic memory, if its spiritual dynamism is loosened from the doctrinal core, that which is powerful becomes dangerous. The history shows much to be commended in Pietist/holiness/Charismatic expressions of Evangelical Christianity; the narrative also reveals reasons to be cautious about some aspects of the spiritual tradition which in contemporary expression are becoming more prominent, perhaps when excessive weight is given to the precise replication of New Testament miracles, or the Spirit is understood in a way that is separate from the Word.

There are two particular challenges to the Charismatic movement today. First, holding firm to the heart of Evangelical spirituality and doctrine. The Word and the cross are central to mainstream Evangelical spirituality. In the quest to be relevant, in the desire to engage the spiritual, to bring Christianity before contemporary society, it is imperative that this dynamism remains biblically doctrinal and does not become simply spiritual entertainment. The first generation of those who came under the powerful influence of Charismatic renewal remained, by and large, expressly committed to Evangelical doctrinal norms. Subsequent generations have been more divided. For some, spirituality trumped doctrine. To be able to lay claim to an authentic Evangelical spirituality, it is not that the reverse is true (doctrine triumphs over spirituality) but that spirituality flows from doctrine. This is the essential direction of travel. Doctrine defines the practice. Spirituality detached from doctrinal norms cannot be an Evangelical spirituality. It is a crucial test. Are our spiritual practices rooted in and flowing from our scriptural and doctrinal norms, or seeking to define new norms? A well-grounded Evangelical spirituality can embrace many of the powerful expressions of faith which neo-Pentecostalism has brought. Equally, there is a responsibility to ensure that spirituality remains rigorous and held within the doctrinal and biblical framework of the Evangelical tradition.

Second, exercising wise discernment in spiritual practice. Tension can arise when spiritual practices take the participant outside of the accepted framework. Some spiritual practices have come to be adopted which have not historically fallen within Evangelical spirituality. We will explore some of these shortly. The real question is how to discern whether a particular practice falls within the historic tradition or is an import from elsewhere. This is not to denigrate the spiritual practices of others; rather to ensure that we have a full understanding of what constitutes Evangelical spirituality. There are a number of tools which might help us. The principle of first- and second-order issues (see below) has often been applied in Reformed teaching, especially in the self-understanding of Anglican Evangelicalism.[1] We may usefully apply the same principle in the adoption of spiritual practices. In doctrinal terms, a first-order issue is one that affects either *authority* or *salvation*. So, for example, a doctrine which denied the atoning sacrifice of Christ upon the cross (the one perfect sacrifice in our place) would be a belief outside of mainstream Evangelicalism. In respect of spiritual practices, the distinction to be drawn is whether the practice *affirms* or *denies* the underlying doctrinal truth. That would constitute a first-order spiritual practice. A spiritual discipline which did neither of those things could responsibly be seen as a custom where a variety of approaches could be seen as authentically Evangelical.

A second method is to assess the biblical context of the practices. Does the spiritual discipline appear in the Scriptures? In what context and to what extent should it be seen as normative? This assessment would ask whether there is continuity in the practice and whether its appearance at the time of Jesus was of a different order to contemporary practice.

The third approach is to ask what place such practices have had in the historic tradition. Has the practice been adopted in the history of Evangelicalism and, if so, in what setting and context, and with what degree of wider acceptance? The purpose of this methodology is not to stifle appropriate variety but to ensure a well-founded Evangelical spirituality. We will now consider some examples, including some of the more controversial practices, to see if we can discern a way forward.

We will consider three groups of examples. Firstly, inward practices versus outward expression. A good example here would be the use of silence in spiritual discipline. This has become more prominent in contemporary Evangelical practice under the increased influence of both Pietism and Pentecostalist emphases. There is no evidence at all that such practice should be seen as a first-order issue. The use of silent prayer is essentially an inward discipline which, as a practice, does not constitute any form of denial of essential doctrine (though, of course, the content of the prayer itself is a matter between the individual and God). There are examples of the use of silence in Scripture and there is no suggestion that this constituted any form of particular apostolic provision.

Within the historic tradition, although the practice has not been particularly prominent, there is similarly no evidence of its lack of acceptance. Hence a reasonable conclusion is that the use of silence would be a second-order spiritual practice upon which a variety of approaches are acceptable. In essence we might be able to apply this to what might be called "inward" disciplines.

Contrast this with outward practices – for example, auricular confession (that is, the private confession of sin to a priest, or perhaps another, and the receipt of absolution). The question is not whether individuals might find auricular confession useful or spiritually powerful (many clearly do), but whether the practice can be seen as authentically Evangelical. Priestly confession and absolution, for most Evangelicals, constitutes a denial (at least potentially) of the atonement. That is not to claim that everyone who takes part in such exercises is explicitly denying the death of Christ for our sins, but that the practice potentially does so. There is a close causal link between the priestly sacrifice at the altar and the transmission of forgiveness to an individual. While recognizing that modern practice is not necessarily reflecting medieval understandings, there is a serious doctrinal issue here for Evangelical spirituality. There is also lack of biblical evidence. In the history of the tradition auricular confession has been seen as clearly outside of acceptable Evangelical practice. The Earl of Shaftesbury referred to the practice as "monstrous".[2] In essence the practice is an outward form which conveys dubious inner reality. Other examples might include the sign of the cross, genuflection, and the use of incense and vestments. Many may indeed find these practices enriching, and they certainly have a place within other spiritual traditions, but they cannot be seen as Evangelical.

The second group of practices to consider consists of scriptural examples which might suggest a variety of practice. Two examples here will suffice for purposes of illustration – retreat and fasting. Withdrawal for prayer has clear scriptural warrant. So does fasting. There is no evidence that these practices carried any special significance and both have featured within the range of spiritual practices adopted by Evangelicals historically, albeit more on the edge than the centre of the tradition. These exercises are neither mandatory nor inappropriate.

Thirdly, we will consider some more controversial areas. We should seek, in dealing with areas of more disputed practice, to avoid polemic, to recognize that which is healthy and good, but to see also if we can find a way to properly assess some common spiritual disciplines. The purpose of this book has been largely to explain variety but also to seek to establish some boundaries and limits.

As an example, let us consider the practice of healing. Does healing point to the salvation offered by Christ? Is the practice of healing an imitation of the ministry of Jesus? And are contemporary healing practices consonant with both biblical and historic practice? For most of the last two thousand years there has been a cautious consensus on these matters, but this has been challenged in contemporary Evangelical spiritual practice. Healing in the New Testament was generally seen as a sign pointing beyond the healing itself to the glory of God. Most, but not all, healings in the New Testament were carried out by Jesus. There is also an instance of Jesus sending out his followers to "preach and heal".

The first question is whether healing constitutes a first-order practice (and hence to be followed or avoided) or a second-order practice (thus permitting a variety of practice).

The complexity is that healing in the New Testament seems to be associated with, but distinguished from, the proclamation of salvation. Healings generally have wider purposes than the healing itself. Cautiously, we might suggest that any contemporary practice of healing needs to be carefully conducted so as not to distract from the proclamation of the gospel. Equally complex is the matter of whether the healings of the New Testament should be replicated today as normative or whether healings in apostolic times carried very specific characteristics which cannot or should not be repeated.

Despite the current penchant for the healing ministry, Evangelicals would here wish to express some caution. The healings of the New Testament were of a different order from contemporary practice. They were sudden, dramatic and extraordinary. They involved raising from the dead, restoring sight, curing lameness and so on. The outcomes were easily verifiable, both medically (though we have no evidence that this was done) and experientially – the one who was blind could now see. Sometimes these practices involved symbolic actions alongside. Although some Charismatic and Pentecostal Christians make similar claims today, mainstream Evangelical spirituality, including Charismatic Evangelicals who advocate and practise healing ministries, would advise prudence in any direct association between apostolic healings and contemporary practice. It is the failure sometimes to exercise such wise discernment that opens the door for extravagant and unjustifiable claims. We should also note that historically healings have occasionally featured within Evangelicalism (at the margins), but until more recently have not been central to Evangelical spirituality.

So what does this imply for the contemporary healing ministry? Clearly there is some biblical warrant. The key lies in recognizing the appropriate place and practice of such ministry (which is deeply valued by many) and ensuring that it does not distract from the gospel and does not make reckless claims. If those criteria are met, within a framework of responsible biblical teaching about well-being and personhood, then the healing ministry can be seen as a second-order spiritual discipline, thus recognizing that Evangelical Christians will adopt a range of practices and positions in connection with the ministry. In that way, the contemporary healing ministry can be maintained within an authentically Evangelical framework. The difficulty arises because a second-order practice can sometimes masquerade as a first-order one, in which case Evangelicals would be considerably more cautious.

There are many other spiritual gifts and practices we could consider in this framework. Some, especially lifestyle issues (e.g. simplicity), would seem to fit within the range of second-order disciplines permitting of a variety of practice within Evangelicalism. However, some of the more extreme lifestyle questions have tended historically to operate on the margins of Pietism, with its emphasis on separation from the world. The Pentecostal and Charismatic traditions have not spoken with one voice on these issues. Some have advocated radical lifestyle changes while others have promoted "health and wealth" approaches to the gospel. Perhaps there is an appropriate caution towards both.

Some of the so-called supernatural gifts (tongues, prophecy) have also generated some controversy. An approach similar to the one adopted with healing might be the most fruitful and lead to a careful and balanced analysis. Perhaps the current practice of prophecy in some parts of the Charismatic Evangelical tradition is the one where there is most discontinuity between apostolic and contemporary practices. Tongues-speaking, on the other hand, although suffering from a lack of historical accreditation, features not only in the New Testament but in a similar way within both classic Pentecostalism and Charismatic renewal. The difference is that in the classic Pentecostalist denominations tongues-speaking has been seen as a mark of salvation – which is almost certainly erroneous – while contemporary Charismatic practice embraces the phenomenon but is more balanced and cautious about its place.

The renewal of Evangelical spirituality

Perhaps the most important question we face, in the light of this assessment, is how to renew Evangelical spirituality today. Now that we have sought to make sense of the historic tradition – its variety, disciplines, practices and challenges – what can be done? "Spirituality" as such is a neutral word; Evangelical spirituality has the potential to be a powerful spiritual force for the renewal of Evangelicalism.

Reclaiming spiritual discipline today

Evangelical Christianity carries the great danger of being theologically fit and spiritually flabby. Discipline is not a popular word and spiritual discipline even less so, and yet there is a yearning and desire for authenticity within Evangelical spirituality. However, it is crucial for us to reassess the key elements of a genuinely dynamic spiritual life and seek to encourage and model such a life for others.

The first discipline to be reclaimed is that of *knowing the Scriptures*. Spirituality without the Bible is barely Christian and certainly not Evangelical. The Bible needs to be recovered and the people of God empowered in their Bible reading. The Bible has become to so many either a closed book or a burden. Without the Word of God in Scripture we cannot fully know him, and certainly not as Redeemer. The first spiritual discipline is that of devotional, private reading of Scripture. The Bible belongs in the hands and heart of the believer and it is the responsibility of church leaders to ensure that the saints of God are equipped with the Word of God. Hence the Bible must be taught. The reading of the Bible must be modelled. The priority of the Bible as the key spiritual and devotional tool of the people of God must be advocated and proclaimed. This will require a new approach to Scripture in our churches. This could perhaps be best summed up as *confidence*, *commitment* and *catechesis*. The Bible needs to feature in worship, in private devotion and in public and private teaching. Confidence needs to be restored, commitment enhanced and catechesis undertaken.

The second spiritual discipline to be recovered is that of a *devotional heart*. This means an enhanced understanding and formation of the heart as turned towards God, glorifying him and submitted to him. Prayer, worship and devotional practice all feature here. Indeed, perhaps it is here that we might see the widest range of personal spiritual practices (methods of praying and formation, styles of worship and singing). In the light of our assessment of how to evaluate such practices, method and style can, by and large, be seen as second-order spiritual issues, provided the focus is on Scripture, devotion and living the Christian life.

Third, we would be well advised to reclaim the concept of *the providential life*. One feature of Evangelical devotional life which seems to have been somewhat lost is the idea of the whole of life being lived under the providential hand of God. This will include, but not be restricted to, seeing God's special and powerful action in our lives. More important, however, is the recognition of growing in grace over the long haul, submitting ourselves to God daily, monthly, yearly, exercising long-term discipline over sin and submitting ourselves ever more to God's ways and purposes. A providential view of the daily Christian life will also encourage Christians to regain confidence in God's providential hand over the universe and public life. Struggle and surrender will both feature; what is most important is for the individual Christian to recognize their dependence upon the Lord as they seek to grow in knowledge of him (Scripture), give their heart to him (prayer and devotion), and live for him faithfully day by day (providence).

The powerful preaching of the Word of God

Our historical review of Evangelical spiritual devotion and practice revealed the importance of preaching and proclamation. Under the influence of the Holy Spirit such setting forth of the Word of God has been the single most important and powerful tool used by God to bring revival.

A revolution is needed in preaching. A transformation, that is, which removes preaching from the cul-de-sacs of both emotional manipulation and lifeless explanation. The preaching of Wesley and Whitefield changed hearts and lives. It was both doctrinal and heart-changing, appealing to the intelligence and the emotions. Genuinely Spirit-filled preaching will teach, train and change hearts. As a consequence of the loss of confidence in Scripture as the Word of God, we see a consequential loss of assurance in the Word proclaimed in the power of the Spirit. Preachers need better training and more focused preparation. They need an absolute confidence in God's Word and a dependency upon him. Today's preachers are to bring God's Word to his people and also to proclaim Christian truth to the outsider. Those that preach need to give a serious priority to the ministry. Their task is to equip the saints for works of service. Significant time needs to be set aside for preparation, and congregations need to be trained in hearing the Word and grasping its significance. That is not an excuse for either a waffling preacher or a sleeping congregation; it is an argument for a shared priority in the centrality of the Word.

However, as well as presenting a challenge to the preachers, a revived and renewed Evangelical spirituality will test the discipline of those who listen to sermons. The people of God need to be assisted in how to listen and learn, how to grow through the weekly feeding of the proclaimed Word, how to digest the food and be nourished. Perhaps as much attention should be paid to the hearers as to the speakers. Preachers should consider providing advance notice of the passage, room for personal notes, encouragement to use personal Bibles, follow-up Bible studies and even question-and-answer sessions after sermons. Perhaps the use of modern technology could provide podcasts, visual aids, notes and so on. Innovation and creativity is the key. Preaching and prayer are also closely related and would benefit from closer attention. Prayer has become detached from the preached Word. Perhaps extempore congregational prayer as a response to the sermon or other innovative methods could be used, or the preacher could provide prayer points for the week. The Word of God should be celebrated, read, digested and obeyed. In that way, under the Spirit, the Word transforms both the speaker and the hearer.

Spirituality and evangelism

Spirituality is sometimes seen as an esoteric concept dealing only with the inward disposition of the heart. Evangelicalism can certainly learn about the importance of quiet, trust and "waiting" upon God. However, Evangelical faith is also active. Hence an authentic Evangelical spirituality must link the inner life of prayer and devotion to the objects of Evangelical action. In other words, a spirituality which does not issue in some manner in evangelism is likely to grow moribund. Devotionally, the starting point is to have a heart for the lost, and this will include prayer for the conversion of specific individuals. This may be accompanied by prayer for a genuine revival – an outpouring of the Spirit of God in which people will come under the saving grace of the gospel in considerable numbers. This orientation helps ensure that spirituality, piety and devotion do not become simply a personal tonic but are an impulse to the spread of the gospel. This will have consequences for our spiritual lives. A concern for world and local mission and evangelism will feature in the Evangelical spiritual life. This may emanate in prayer and financial support for the missionary enterprise, both individually and as part of the corporate life of a church. Similarly, we might expect to see some weight given to ministries of mercy and transformation within the devotional life of the believer.

Spirituality and service

A key element of our explorations in this book focused around conversion and call. The power of both is underplayed in contemporary Evangelical spirituality. The autonomy of the self, the advance of rationality and the quest for the mystical have all served to lessen the emphasis on this key building-block of Evangelical spirituality. Not only does conversion need to be back on the agenda but also the consequence of conversion – call. The offering of our lives in sacrificial Christian service does not derive from duty or responsibility or even from spiritual experiences, but flows essentially from our status as converted beings before God. A significantly greater affirmation of the calling of the Christian to service – in life, in business, in occupation, in vocation – would firmly root Evangelical spirituality in its Reformed origins. Particular weight may be given to the call to the Christian life in public service. We have noted inspirational role models from the past and these serve as powerful models for today. All Christians, whether in public service or private enterprise, need to be encouraged and supported in their private piety. There may be a particular spiritual calling on some to support in prayer those called into the public square. The key is to recognize that the inner spirituality of the Evangelical must have a practical outworking in evangelism and service.

Notes

1. Richard Turnbull, *Anglican and Evangelical?*, London: Continuum, 2007 (reprinted 2010), pp. 101–103.
2. E. Hodder, *The Life and Work of the Seventh Earl of Shaftesbury*, 3 volumes, London: Cassell & Company, 1887, volume 1, p. 333.

Conclusion

....

We have journeyed round the contours of Evangelical spirituality, looking for roots and connections. We have sought to explain the sources, the emphases and the development of the various strands of the Evangelical spiritual tradition. In doing so the aim has been to increase understanding but also to recover the spiritual vitality of Evangelical faith. In Scripture, conversion, call, prayer, providence and revival we have sought to discover the heart of this spirituality. We have considered inspiring figures, those whose transformed hearts changed their lives. We have also looked at the cul-de-sacs, the detours down which Evangelicals who have lost their foundations and roots may sometimes travel. We have sought to provide some tools to assist the believer to assess spiritual practices with balance, wisdom and discernment.

We need to make no apology for the aim of regaining for Evangelical spirituality an emphasis on the traditional disciplines of Bible, prayer, the Christian life, evangelism and service. For the Evangelical the outward form of spirituality is action. There remains much to learn about the inward disciplines and an appreciation of the variety of approaches within the tradition. At the core of Evangelical spirituality lies a converted heart, a life lived under the providence of God and a passion for his glory, his holiness, his gospel and his service.

Select Bibliography

Aitken, Jonathan, *John Newton*, London: Continuum, 2007.

Anstey, Roger, *The Atlantic Slave Trade and British Abolition*, London: Macmillan, 1975.

Bebbington, David, *Evangelicalism in Modern Britain*, London: Unwin Hyman, 1989.

Bebbington, David, *The Dominance of Evangelicalism*, Leicester: IVP, 2005.

Best, Gary, *Charles Wesley*, Peterborough: Epworth, 2006.

Bradley, Ian, *Abide With Me*, London: SCM Press, 1997.

Calvin, John, *Institutes of the Christian Religion*, 1559, Library of Christian Classics, ed. J. T. McNeil, 2 volumes, Philadelphia: Westminster Press, 1960.

Clark, J. C. D., *English Society 1688-1832*, Cambridge: CUP, 1985.

Cook, Faith, *Selina, Countess of Huntingdon*, Edinburgh: Banner of Truth Trust, 2001.

Gatiss, Lee (ed.), *The Sermons of George Whitefield*, 2 volumes, Watford: Church Society, 2010.

George, Timothy (ed.), *Mr Moody and the Evangelical Tradition*, London and New York: Continuum, 2004.

Gordon, James, *Evangelical Spirituality*, London: SPCK, 1991.

Grubb, Norman, *C. T. Studd*, London: Religious Tract Society, 1933.

Hague, William, *William Wilberforce*, London: Harper Perennial, 2008.

Hennell, M. M. and Pollard, A. (eds), *Charles Simeon (1759-1836)*, London: SPCK, 1959.

Hindmarsh, D. Bruce, *The Evangelical Conversion Narrative*, Oxford: OUP, 2005.

Jones C., Wainwright G. and Yarnold E., *The Study of Spirituality*, London: SPCK, 6th impression, 2004.

Kenny, A. (ed.), *Wycliffe in his Times*, Oxford: Clarendon Press, 1986.

Kidd, Thomas S., *The Great Awakening*, New Haven: Yale University Press, 2007.

Murray, Iain, *Revival and Revivalism*, Edinburgh: Banner of Truth Trust, 1994.

Mursell, G., *English Spirituality, From Earliest Times to 1700*, London: SPCK, 2008.

Newport, Kenneth G. C. and Campbell, Ted A. (eds), *Charles Wesley: Life, Literature and Legacy*, Peterborough: Epworth, 2007.

Newsome, D., *The Parting of Friends*, London: John Murray, 1966.

Noll, Mark, *The Rise of Evangelicalism*, Leicester: Apollos, 2004.

Packer, J. I., *Knowing God*, Downers Grove, Illinois: IVP, 20th anniversary edition, 1993.

Porter, R. and Teich, M., *The Enlightenment in National Context*, Cambridge: CUP, 1981.

Pratt, J. H., *The Thought of the Evangelical Leaders*, 1856, Edinburgh: Banner of Truth Trust, 1978.

Rack, Henry, *Reasonable Enthusiast*, London: Epworth, 1989.

Robinson, James, *Pentecostal Origins*, Milton Keynes: Paternoster, 2005.

Rosman, D., *Evangelicals and Culture*, Beckenham: Croon Helm, 1984.

Ryle, J. C., *Holiness*, London: James Clark and Co., 1956.

Tiller, J., *Puritan, Pietist, Pentecostalist: Three Types of Evangelical Spirituality*, Nottingham: Grove Books, 1982.

Turnbull, Richard, *Anglican and Evangelical?*, London: Continuum, 2007 (reprinted 2010).

Turnbull, Richard, *Shaftesbury: The Great Reformer*, Oxford: Lion, 2010.

Turnbull, Richard, *Reviving the Heart: The Story of the Eighteenth Century Revival*, Oxford: Lion, 2012.

Warrington, K. (ed.), *Pentecostal Perspectives*, Carlisle: Paternoster Press, 1998.

Wolffe, J., *The Expansion of Evangelicalism*, Leicester: IVP, 2006.

Yancey, Philip, *Prayer*, London: Hodder and Stoughton, 2006.

Index